Scripture quotations marked (NIV) are taken from the Holy Bible, New International Version®, NIV®. Copyright © 1973, 1978, 1984, 2011 by Biblica, Inc.™ Used by permission of Zondervan. All rights reserved worldwide. www.zondervan.comThe "NIV" and "New International Version" are trademarks registered in the United States Patent and Trademark Office by Biblica, Inc.™

Scripture quotations marked (NKJV) are taken from the New King James Version®. Copyright © 1982 by Thomas Nelson. Used by permission. All rights reserved.

Scripture quotations marked (NASB) are taken from the (NASB®) New American Standard Bible®, Copyright © 1960, 1971, 1977, 1995, 2020 by The Lockman Foundation. Used by permission. All rights reserved. lockman.org

Scripture quotations marked (NLT) are taken from the Holy Bible, New Living Translation, copyright ©1996, 2004, 2015 by Tyndale House Foundation. Used by permission of Tyndale House Publishers, Carol Stream, Illinois 60188. All rights reserved.

Scripture quotations marked (ESV) are taken from The ESV® Bible (The Holy Bible, English Standard Version®), © 2001 by Crossway, a publishing ministry of Good News Publishers. Used by permission. All rights reserved.

Scripture referenced from The King James Version (KJV) are in the public domain and have been used in reverence to those who spent their lives translating the Word.

hb
hope✷books

Table of Contents

Foreword vii

About the Chapters ix

Chapter 1
Glimmers in the Web: A Journey Through
Cancer and Light
By *Kalindi L. Garvin* 1

Chapter 2
Fear Doesn't Get the Final Say: Reframing
Fear in Remission
By *Heather Hetchler, MA* 11

Chapter 3
Trust Your Gut and the Holy Spirit
By *Page Geske* 31

Chapter 4
God's Grace in the Waiting: Faith Refined
Through Suffering
By *Amy McClain* 47

Chapter 5
Cancer Sucks, But Your Life Doesn't Have To!
By *Julie Stapleton* 67

Chapter 6
Scary Doctor
By *Susan Laurie Hutchinson* 75

~ v ~

Chapter 7
A Divine Orchestration: My Journey Through Fear,
Faith, and Healing
By Julie O'Dell 93

Chapter 8
The Power of Adaptability: Surviving the Battle
from Both Sides
By Dr. Charrisse Somme-Davis 109

Chapter 9
My Battle with Breast Cancer: From Survivor
to Thriver, from Dandelion to Iris
By Deborah (Debbie) Jenkins 117

About the Authors 127

Closing 138

Foreword

By Hope H. Dover

Cancer touches more than just the body. It reaches into the moments we thought would be ordinary, into the spaces we never expected to be sacred. It changes routines, reshapes relationships, and redefines what strength really looks like.

Beyond the Battle is a collection of stories from survivors who have walked through the unimaginable and come out the other side. Perhaps not the same, but still standing. These are not stories tied up in bows or filled with easy answers. They are honest, layered, and tender. They speak to the pain, the fear, and the uncertainty, but also to the faith, resilience, and unshakable hope that rises in the hardships.

Each chapter is a testimony of survival, but also of what it means to live fully, even when the future feels fragile. Whether you're in the fight yourself, walking alongside someone you love, or simply trying to make sense of your own story, my hope is that you'll find something here that helps you breathe a little deeper and feel a little less alone.

We hope these stories meet you right where you are and remind you that healing isn't just found in the cure. It's also found in the connection, the courage, and the community of others who understand.

Hope and healing don't always arrive the way we imagined. Sometimes, they show up in a shared story. That's what this book is—a collection of sacred, hard-won stories to remind us that even beyond the battle, there is still so much life to be lived.

About the Chapters

Kalindi L. Garvin opens the collection with a reflection on her journey with early-onset colorectal cancer. She weaves together the beauty of ordinary life with the reality of treatment and survivorship. From the quiet presence of spiderwebs on a morning walk to the challenge of parenting through illness, Kalindi invites us to notice the glimmers of grace hidden in even the hardest days.

In chapter 2, Heather Hetchler, MA vulnerably shares how fear lingers long after treatment ends. Through personal story and faith-filled reflection, she normalizes post-treatment anxiety and offers practical tools for reframing fear, replacing it with truth, and anchoring your heart in God's promises.

Page Geske's story in "Trust Your Gut and the Holy Spirit" is a powerful reminder to listen to your body and the prompting of the Holy Spirit. Diagnosed with colon cancer after trusting her intuition, Page testifies to God's provision and healing. Her chapter is both a call to action and a testament to the faithfulness of community.

In her chapter, Amy McClain shares her story of serving as a missionary in Papua when a thyroid cancer diagnosis interrupted everything. Through her deep wrestling with disappointment and trust, Amy reveals how grace and spiritual transformation can emerge through life's most unexpected detours.

With honesty and humor, Julie Stapleton walks through her experience with HER2+ breast cancer in chapter 5. From diagnosis to chemotherapy to surgery, Julie reminds us that cancer is hard—but life can still be beautiful. Her words offer hope, encouragement, and practical advice for those facing their own battle.

In "Scary Doctor," Susan Laurie Hutchinson tells the story of her stage 4 ovarian cancer diagnosis with wit, wisdom, and vulnerability. What begins as fear becomes faith as Susan learns to shift her trust from the words of her doctor to the promises of God. This is a testimony of strength, worship, and profound hope.

In chapter 7, Julie O'Dell shares her miraculous story of healing from a rare abdominal tumor. From the moment of diagnosis to the unexpected intervention of a stranger, Julie's story is a powerful witness to God's orchestration, the power of prayer, and the courage to trust the still, small voice within.

Dr. Charrisse Somme-Davis writes from the unique perspective of both caregiver and survivor in chapter 8. Drawing from her experience as a therapist and her father's caregiver, Charrisse highlights the importance of mindset, support, and faith in navigating cancer's disruption and claiming resilience.

Deborah (Debbie) Jenkins closes the collection by sharing her journey with breast cancer through the lens of anxiety, faith, and transformation. Her chapter gently acknowledges the emotional and physical toll of cancer while pointing toward thriving beyond survival. Like the iris, Debbie's story blooms with hope and purpose.

Chapter 1

Glimmers in the Web: A Journey Through Cancer and Light

By Kalindi L. Garvin

"TO PAY ATTENTION, THIS IS OUR ENDLESS AND PROPER WORK"
- MARY OLIVER[1]

The morning unfurled like silk, warm and heavy with summer. My two Goldendoodles trotted ahead, tails high, looking back at me every few steps to make sure I followed. The mown trail curved gently through the grass, dew gathering on my shoes with each step. I walked slowly, letting the sun press against my skin, the air thick with the green sweetness of growing things.

It was early—the kind of early that asks for silence—and I welcomed it. These walks had become my steadying ritual, the one thread of myself I could still trace amid the unraveling.

---

1 Mary Oliver, "Yes! No!," in *Owls and Other Fantasies: Poems and Essays* (Beacon Press, 2003), 27.

And then, I saw them.

Spiderwebs glinted between blades of grass and branches—so many, almost too many to count. Each one was draped in dew, glistening in the slant of morning sun like shards of glass flung from a hidden chandelier. I paused, breath caught in my throat. Had they always been there, these jeweled threads? Had I simply never noticed?

I reached for my phone instinctively. But then I stopped. This wasn't meant to be captured. It was meant to be witnessed.

And in that stillness, a knowing came over me—clear, simple, whole.

My life was like these webs. Strung with invisible threads no one else could see—fatigue that hollowed my bones, a body that no longer obeyed, a quiet ache beneath the surface. And yet, there was beauty too. Even in the breaking, something luminous remained.

"To pay attention, this is our endless and proper work"
- Mary Oliver[2]

And on that morning, I did. I paid attention. I saw the glimmers. And they saw me.

But even moments like that dissolve quickly when the world tilts.

When the Web Tightened

I knew before I opened it. The test results were waiting, but so was the truth I wasn't ready to face. My hands trembled

---

2 Oliver, *Owls and Other Fantasies*, 27.

as I fumbled with the facial recognition on my phone, barely able to log into MyChart. My mom and I sat at Biaggi's, one of our favorite restaurants, waiting for my shrimp and salmon risotto. The clink of silverware, the soft din of conversation, the sun filtering through the windows—it all felt too normal to contain the weight of what I was about to read.

It had started so routinely—a colonoscopy in January. Just a box to check. A preventive measure. But within days, my chart had transformed from "no known allergies, no medications" to "stage three early-onset colorectal cancer."

Appointments poured in: bloodwork, MRIs, surgery consults. My search history ballooned with terrifying terms: survival rates, chemotherapy side effects, how to tell your kids you have cancer.

I bought a red floral binder and filled it with color-coded tabs. Appointments. Notes. Questions. Insurance forms. It gave me something tangible, a way to pretend control was still possible.

But control was a fragile illusion.

The hardest part? I didn't look sick. No hollow cheeks. No head scarf. No visible cue to signal what was growing inside me. I looked like myself, but felt like a stranger. As if I'd wandered into a film I didn't audition for and was playing the middle-aged mom with cancer.

How would I afford treatment—on top of groceries, car repairs, and keeping teenagers clothed, fed, and emotionally afloat? Who would take the new puppy out? Would I have the strength to keep up with everything—work, appointments, late-night talks?

The vision of my independence blurred and darkened. I was no longer sure I could do it all. And more than that, I was afraid of what might happen if I couldn't.

The Weaving of Daily Life

I bought a bouquet of stargazer lilies before surgery and placed them by my bed. I wanted something beautiful waiting for me when I got home. Their scent—sweet, insistent—reminded me I was still here.

Life carried on, as life does, filled with in-service days and ortho appointments, tire rotations, and birthday gifts. I made a playlist for infusion days. I downloaded cancer meditations on the *Calm* mindfulness app, trying to steady the storm inside me. I read Mary Oliver's poems with the reverence of scripture. I made lists to keep the chaos at bay: CT scans. Chemo pump removal days. Bloodwork. Nausea logs.

I booked a massage before my third round of chemo. As I lay beneath warm blankets, I told the therapist about my diagnosis. She didn't speak. She simply rested her hands gently on my forehead—thumbs still, palms warm. In that silence, I felt something sacred pass between us.

Even now, I carry that moment.

The Boat Ride that Loosened the Knot

By midsummer, cancer had consumed everything—my time, my energy, my peace. Treatment had left me raw, exhausted, and running to the bathroom more times a day than I could count.

There had been moments earlier that summer that shook me more than I let on—like the night I ended up in the

ER, bleeding from surgery, my hemoglobin so low they were preparing for a possible transfusion. I remember answering my daughter's text from the hospital bed. "When are you coming home?" she asked. I told her not to worry, that I just had to stay overnight so they could check a few things. I softened my tone, added a heart emoji, anything to make it sound routine.

I didn't want to scare her. I didn't want to cause my kids any more anxiety than they already carried. They were teenagers navigating their own lives—school, friendships, the invisible pressures of growing up—and I didn't want cancer to be yet another weight on their shoulders.

Parenting through illness became its own private burden. Every appointment, every hospital stay, every side effect—I wasn't just enduring it for myself. I was managing their experience of it too. Trying to keep their lives steady, their days normal.

Then my parents invited me on a boat ride.

It was a perfect 75-degree day—the kind where the air feels soft and golden, where the lake lies still and shimmering like a sheet of glass. I wanted to go. I really did. But the thought of being stranded on the water without a bathroom filled me with quiet panic. I hesitated. I almost said no.

And then my parents found a solution: a Luggable Loo and a pop-up tent. They told me, gently but firmly, "If you need it, it'll be there." So I went.

As the boat pulled away from the dock, something inside me began to loosen. The tension I'd been carrying seeped into the water with every gentle ripple. For a few precious hours, the pressure of cancer receded. I wasn't a patient. I wasn't battling anything or managing symptoms. I was just a daughter, afloat with her parents, watching the horizon stretch wide and open.

In that space, something became clear. Cancer had taken so much, but it had also clarified what mattered most. The quiet, ordinary moments that make a life: bedtime hugs and late-night laughter, quick coffee stops after orthodontist appointments, long drives filled with silence and music.

The choice to say yes to time together.

To keep showing up and to love as fully as I could, even on the hardest days.

My greatest purpose had always been right in front of me—my kids, my family, the people I love. They were the reason I kept going. The reason I softened the edges of the truth. The reason I fought so fiercely to stay.

And in the midst of that love, I still found meaning in my work—the conversations, the impact, the seeds planted that might bloom long after I'm gone. Work wasn't just a job; it was an extension of my care, my creativity, my commitment to making things better for others.

I gave what I could, even when I didn't know how. I kept looking for beauty, even when things got hard.

The Tangle Unwinds

I know I had it easier than many. I still had two more rounds of chemo ahead of me when my scans came back clear. No lymph node involvement. The moment I saw the results, I called my oncologist, grateful for a window between meetings so I could close my office door and sit with the news.

Relief washed over me, but it was laced with disbelief. I could skip the final treatments and transition to a "watch and wait": trading chemo appointments for bloodwork, scans, and monitoring. Just like that, I was done.

It felt surreal to be "back to normal," like I'd crash-landed on Earth after living on another planet. My body had changed. My life had changed. But the world around me hadn't paused. It kept moving as if nothing had happened.

How was I supposed to return to life as it was? Was I even meant to?

After all the guidance on navigating treatment, there was surprisingly little about what comes next.

What I didn't realize—and what no one really prepares you for—is how survivorship is not an ending. It's another beginning, but one that comes without clear markers, timelines, or milestones. There's no bell to ring. Just a calendar of scan dates and a body that feels like it's still whispering, *Be careful. Don't forget what we've been through.*

People meant well. They said, "You must be so relieved!" or "Now you can finally move on." I smiled and nodded. But inside, I didn't feel finished. I felt ... suspended. Fragile. Hollowed out. Exhausted.

I returned to work carrying both deep gratitude and quiet pressure. At first, I eased back into a familiar role, trying to find my footing again, trying to remember who I was outside of chemo appointments and scan results. Then, a year after being declared cancer-free, I stepped into something new.

The role came with more responsibility, more visibility, and a sense of purpose I was eager to embrace. I wanted to show up fully. To prove I was capable. To build something that mattered. But I was doing it all with a body still aching from radiation, still adjusting to hormonal shifts, still carrying the weight of daily fear.

There's this unspoken expectation that you'll "bounce back"—as if healing has a deadline. But real healing is quieter, messier, slower. It's realizing you need to sit down halfway up the stairs. It's reaching for Advil or crying in the car or skipping one more social thing because your reserves are empty.

Nearly eighteen months have passed since that clean scan. I wish I could say the fear vanished the day they said remission, but it didn't. I still overanalyze every new ache or delayed test result. There's no roadmap for this. No checklist. Just the slow, uncertain work of redefining "normal."

But here's what I know: Survivorship isn't about bouncing back, it's about growing forward. It's not about reclaiming your old self—it's about becoming someone new, rooted in the same soul but shaped by what you've lived through.

And maybe that's where the glimmers come in. In the threads we use to mend ourselves, we weave our lives together one luminous moment at a time.

The Shadow of the Threads

Earlier this year, my port was removed. My mom sat beside me, just like she did for my colonoscopy, my scans, my first infusion. We had come full circle.

As the doctor pulled the port from my chest, I felt the tug—not just of skin, but of memory. It had lived beneath my skin for so long, a quiet anchor of survival.

Another web. Another thread. And then it was gone.

Later that week, I walked the trail again. The morning was still and gray. No dew sparkled on the grass. No webs caught the light. But I didn't feel disappointed. I knew they were there, strung quietly between the branches, waiting for the right light to reveal them.

Survivorship feels like that. You can't always see the threads that hold you together. But they're there. Just beneath the surface. Just waiting.

And so am I.

Reflective Prompt

Take a walk. Look for what glimmers around you—small moments of beauty, grace, or clarity. Let yourself see what you might normally pass by. Then write down what you noticed and how it made you feel.

The glimmers are always there—waiting, like the webs, for those willing to notice.

Chapter 2
Fear Doesn't Get the Final Say: Reframing Fear in Remission

By Heather Hetchler, MA

TRUST IN THE LORD WITH ALL YOUR HEART AND LEAN NOT ON YOUR OWN UNDERSTANDING; IN ALL YOUR WAYS SUBMIT TO HIM, AND HE WILL MAKE YOUR PATHS STRAIGHT.

PROVERBS 3:5-6 (NIV)

I thought ringing the bell would release all my fears. Instead, fear changed shape, wrapping itself in new thoughts as I sat quietly beside my husband on the drive home from my last radiation treatment.

Looking at him later that night, I remember asking, "Can you build an MRI machine in the doorway of our bedroom? That way, every time I walk through it in the morning, it beeps and says, 'Heather, you're clear.'"

I was only half-joking.

He chuckled, shaking his head, but I could see the concern in his eyes. "I wish I could, babe," he said softly.

That's when I realized— he couldn't give me what I craved. No one could. Certainty. Reassurance. The ability to declare, once and for all, that I had won the battle never to be fought again.

The words *cancer-free* were supposed to be the finish line, the moment I could breathe again. But instead, I found myself battling something no one warned me about—the endless *what-ifs* that came after treatment ended.

When you're in the thick of cancer, everything revolves around the next appointment, the next treatment, the next decision. You have a roadmap. There's structure. Even though it's hard, there's a plan.

And then, suddenly, you're done.

They tell you you're fine and to move on. They give you an appointment card for six months in the future. But how do you move on when every follow-up scan, every ache, every moment of fatigue makes you wonder if it's coming back?

I remember flipping my planner over and seeing my first post-treatment follow-up appointment written in black ink. My stomach clenched. I felt physically sick. *What if it's back? What if the bloodwork catches something this time?*

I never felt the cancer when it was inside me, so how would I know if it had returned? That's when I realized: cancer may have left my body, but the *fear* of it returning was still inside.

Surgeons remove cancer, but only God can quiet fear.

Reframing Fear in Remission

You've made it through surgery. You've finished treatment. Maybe you rang the bell, maybe you didn't. You've likely heard the words 'cancer-free'—but that doesn't mean the fear is gone.

What often goes unspoken is what happens next. No one warns you how a scene in a movie can suddenly stir panic. How a new ache can steal your breath and send your mind racing. How a song that lifts others' spirits can break you wide open.

For many of us, the fear doesn't leave when the cancer does. It lingers. Sometimes quietly in the background, other times right there in front of you, impossible to ignore. If you've felt that shadow of fear follow you into remission, I want you to know—you're not alone.

You can be sitting with a warm cup of coffee one minute, feeling grateful, and the next, tears are streaming down your face. It doesn't always make sense. But it does. Fear and gratitude coexist. Anxiety weaves through peace. That's not a failure of faith, it's a natural response to the trauma and survival mode a cancer diagnosis and treatment bring.

So what do you *do* with that fear?

You sit with it. You honor it. You remind yourself that feeling fear doesn't mean something is wrong with you. It means you're human. It means you've been through something that shook your world.

In the pages ahead, I'll share simple but transformative tips to help you navigate fear—because while fear may still show up, it doesn't have to take over. This isn't about denying your fear. It's about taking it captive and holding it up to the light of God's truth. Letting His peace speak louder than the what-ifs.

Normalize Fear in Remission

When I was early in my cancer remission, fear was part of the background noise. Most days, I kept moving, kept smiling, doing what everyone expected. But there were quiet moments when it caught me off guard.

Every day, things started to look different.

I'd notice moms with their kids in the school parking lot or at a coffee shop — and wonder, *Will I be there to see my children graduate from high school and college? Will I get to sit with them at a cafe years from now, hearing about their lives?*

Other times, I'd catch a glimpse of a young couple in love and find myself weeping, whispering desperate prayers to God to let me grow old with my husband.

I didn't say those fears out loud. Honestly, I didn't even like admitting them to myself. But they were there, quietly stealing little pieces of the present.

The truth is, it's easy to believe that fear has no place in your remission story. You've been cleared. The hard part is supposed to be over—or at least, that's what people say, and what many of us want to believe.

But fear doesn't get the memo.

When the appointments stop and you're released with hugs and cheers, you may find yourself in unfamiliar silence. The routines shift, and the familiar check-ins fade away. In that stillness, it's easy for anxiety, doubt, grief, and worry to rise. If you've felt that disorienting shift, you're not broken or weak — you're healing. That fear you feel isn't failure. It's the echoes of a journey your body and spirit are still processing.

One minute you're going about your day, and the next—a certain smell, a waiting room, or a voicemail reminding you of an upcoming appointment—and you're suddenly back in the emotional space of diagnosis and active treatment.

I'll never forget taking my son in for an MRI on his labrum. We walked into the waiting room, and without even realizing it, I was standing in the exact spot where I once waited for my own MRI-guided biopsy. I froze. My chest tightened. My breath disappeared.

At that moment, I realized something: it was normal. I wasn't broken. I was safe. As I closed my eyes and took a deep breath, I prayed, asking God to calm my heart.

You might notice yourself holding your breath before a scan or racing to worst-case scenarios when a new ache appears. You may feel scared, worried, or tearful for no "good" reason.

When fear shows up, take a deep breath and say this out loud:

"It's normal to feel fear. I can be grateful for my health and still worry about cancer's return."

Write it down. Tape it to your mirror. Speak it over yourself every day if you need to. Fear may be an uninvited visitor, but you don't have to let it move in — you can meet it with truth.

Friend, I've shared my fears with countless survivors, and time and again, I've been met with the same quiet words: "Me too." Many of them thought they were the only ones still carrying these silent fears. But here's the thing: fear loses its power when we name it, when we bring it into the light. When we process it instead of letting it fester in silence.

If fear has you feeling stuck or caught off guard, try this exercise. Find a quiet space and take a sheet of paper. Draw a line down the middle. On the left side, list the losses you've experienced: physical, emotional, relational, spiritual. Beneath those, name any lingering fears: recurrence, future scans, being a burden, or the strain on relationships. Allow yourself to take your time. There's no right or wrong way to do this.

On the right side, write down what's true right now. Truths that stand firm even when fear and doubt cloud your mind. What do you know deep down, regardless of how you feel at this moment? What does your oncologist say? What support systems are in place to carry you through? What does your faith say to you today, even if it's just a quiet whisper of hope?

Sit with both sides. Honor what's been lost. Honor what's uncertain. Reflect on what is true. Simply be present with yourself, without judgment. Please note, this exercise will be different for every survivor. Know that *your* experience is valid and worthy of compassion not comparison.

Fear is a normal part of walking by faith. When Peter stepped out of the boat toward Jesus, he was doing something brave—but when he saw the wind and waves, fear rushed in and he began to sink (Matthew 14:30, NIV). His fear didn't mean he had failed; it meant he was human and he felt scared when he saw the storm.

In the same way, fear can rise in your journey too. When test results take longer than expected, when numbers come back too high or too low, or when you sense something isn't right. Fear will come. But like Peter, you aren't called to stay stuck in it.

When fear rises, don't rush past it. Pause and breathe. Ask yourself, *"What is true right now?"* Let the answers come slowly: *I am here. I am healing. I am not alone.* Say the words out loud if you choose, and let them anchor you. The goal isn't to erase fear—it's to meet it with truth. It's to name what is real and remember that fear doesn't have the final word.

The presence of fear doesn't cancel out the presence of God.

And this is where *reframing* comes in, not by denying fear, but by viewing it through the lens of God's truth. It gives us language for our emotions, and it offers a steady light when fear tries to cloud our vision.

Truth to Anchor You

"When I am afraid, I put my trust in You." Psalm 56:3 (NIV)

Scripture doesn't shame us for being afraid. It's clear that fear will come—not if, but when.

You don't have to pretend fear isn't real. You simply get to choose where to place it. And when fear comes, place your trust in the One who never changes, even when everything else feels uncertain.

Reframe the Fear

At my one-year check-up, my oncologist ordered a biopsy on a concerning spot he'd been monitoring. The moment he said it, I felt my heart race and my stomach tighten with dread. I managed to calm my fears leading up to the actual biopsy. But waiting on the results was a different story.

Five days passed with no call. The silence was unbearable, and my mind raced with worst-case scenarios. I'd been through biopsies before, and in my experience, delays often meant something had been found and was being typed. Logically, I knew that wasn't always true, but fear isn't logical. Fear whispered, "*This is bad.*"

Then, on the fifth day, I was scrolling through Instagram to distract myself when I came across a post from a friend: "*God is good, my husband is cancer-free.*" In that moment, something shifted. I thought, "*I need to declare that God is good—right now, not just if my results are good.*" It hit me: trust wasn't about the outcome. It was about choosing peace in the waiting. Trusting God when I didn't have all the answers. While the waiting didn't get easier overnight, reframing my perspective brought me something valuable—peace in the uncertainty.

Here's what was really happening:

- The feeling: "*The cancer must be back because the doctor still hasn't called.*"
- The fact: "*I had a biopsy. I am waiting for the results.*"
- The fact: "*My past experiences are feeding my fear, but that doesn't guarantee a bad outcome.*"
- The fact: "*I'm scared. And that's okay.*"

Reframing in that moment might sound like this: "It's completely normal to feel anxious while waiting for results. But today, I am healthy. I can be afraid and be ok. God has carried me through hard things before, and He will carry me again. I choose to trust Him with the unknown."

Reframing fear through God's word is like hitting pause, taking a deep breath, and asking yourself, *"Is this fear speaking right now, or is this the truth?"* What and who you choose to listen to will shape how you experience things. Reframing isn't about pretending the fear doesn't exist — it's about intentionally choosing a different lens to view it. It's about shifting your perspective so you can experience the situation differently. Seeing it through God's unwavering truth instead of the shaky lens of fear.

When the fear of cancer returning makes an appearance, you can choose to view it through the lens of God's presence. Isaiah 41:10 (NIV) reminds us: *"So do not fear, for I am with you; do not be dismayed, for I am your God. I will strengthen you and help you; I will uphold you with my righteous right hand."* This verse reframes our fear because God is with us in the waiting, in the uncertainty, and in those moments when doubt threatens to take over.

You can absolutely acknowledge your fear, but you don't have to let it define your story. Instead, hold tightly to the truth that God is your strength. Even when everything feels uncertain, trust that He is holding you with His righteous right hand, offering you peace and courage no matter what comes next.

This reframing process shifts your focus from the fear of the unknown to the solid reassurance of God's constant support. It helps you see fear from a different angle, and when you see it differently, you experience it differently. You're not pretending the fear isn't there, you're simply choosing to look at it through the lens of God's truth. That small shift—even just in a moment—can make a huge difference in how you walk through the day.

Want to try putting this into practice? Grab a piece of paper and write down a recurring fear you often face. Maybe it's something like, *"I'm worried my cancer is back because I'm so tired."* Next, write down the facts—what you actually know to be true: *"I've had a scan, fatigue can come from many things, and I don't have results yet."* Then, bring God's truth into it. Tell yourself, *"Today, I am healthy. God is with me and will be with me in whatever comes. I choose to trust in His peace, even when I don't have all the answers."*

Reframing doesn't change the reality of scans, appointments, or uncertain outcomes, but it helps you navigate those moments with peace and trust. And once you've started to reframe your fear, you can take it a step further by replacing it with the unwavering truth of who God is.

Truth to Anchor You

> *"Do not conform to the pattern of this world, but be transformed by the renewing of your mind."*
>
> Romans 12:2 (NIV)

Fear may speak loudly, but God's truth speaks louder. And His Word invites you to reframe, not ignore your fear, with the hope and peace only He can give. This verse reminds us that transformation happens through the renewing of our minds. And sometimes, that renewal begins with the smallest shift:

From "*What if it's bad?*"

To "*Even if it's hard, God will be with me.*"

As you reframe your thoughts, you can take the next step in replacing fear with the powerful truth found in God's word, allowing His promises to anchor you through even the most uncertain moments.

Replace the Fear

As a survivor, I became hyper-aware of my body. Any new ache or pain would send my mind spiraling into worst-case scenarios—was it a relapse? Something new? What if this was the end? It felt like a constant mental tug-of-war, and honestly, it was exhausting.

In those moments, fear clashed with the well-wishes and cards lined up on my dresser, reminding me how happy I should be that treatment was over and that I could "get back to normal." But here's the truth: there's life before cancer, and then there's life after. Life doesn't go back to the way it was, not completely.

Friends and family, who hadn't walked through cancer themselves, just couldn't fully grasp what I was feeling. And as much as I wanted them to understand, I prayed they never would.

While I didn't have people around me who could fully relate to my struggle, what I did have was God's presence. He got it. His truth became my lifeline. I learned to lean on Scripture, finding specific verses I could stand on—verses I could sleep on and weep on. And the beautiful thing is, you have that available too.

When fear entered my mind, I learned not to panic. Instead, I saw it as an invitation to pause. Rather than letting fear control me, I started practicing a simple yet powerful act: taking that fear captive. I would examine it, reframe it, and replace it with the truth of who God is and what He says about me.

You've already recognized that fear is normal and reframed it through the lens of God's Word. Now, it's time to replace it with the truth of who He is and what He says about you. This is a daily discipline—one that can carry you not just through remission, but through every area of your life.

Negative thoughts, doubts, fears—whatever form they take—can be answered with truth. It might look like standing in front of the mirror on a rough morning and saying: *"For God has not given us a spirit of fear, but of power and of love and of a sound mind."* (2 Timothy 1:7 NKJV)

It might mean writing Scripture on a sticky note and putting it on your steering wheel. It might sound like whispering, *"Jesus, I trust You,"* when your chest tightens at night.

It might be placing your hand on your heart and saying, *"I'm safe. I'm in Your hands. You hold me."* And then, allow yourself to rest in the peace and promise only God can provide.

These may seem like small actions, but they are not small. They are *weapons*. This is a spiritual war, and you are not unarmed. When Satan tempted Jesus in the wilderness, Jesus didn't argue. He didn't explain. He simply answered: "It is written: 'Man shall not live on bread alone, but on every word that comes from the mouth of God.'" (Matthew 4:4, NIV)

I've learned to intentionally slow down with a simple practice that helps me reset when fear makes an unwelcome appearance. I fill my electric kettle with water, turn it on, and then pick out a pretty teacup from my kitchen shelf. While the water is brewing, I choose a tea. Then I pour the boiling water over the tea bag, sit down with my journal and Bible, and let it steep for about seven minutes. It's a small but meaningful ritual that helps me reset.

During that time, my focus is on the physical actions of making tea—on the warmth, the smell, and the process itself. It helps me slow my mind and body and engage with God in a way that makes space for peace. This simple practice allows me to take a thought or fear captive.

Maybe this is something you could try, or maybe there's something else that works for you to help slow down and pause your thoughts. The key is to create space to recognize fear for what it is and replace it with truth.

The thing is, you don't have to argue with fear. You don't need to match its intensity or justify your hope. You just need to stand firm on what is written.

Let God's promises become the soundtrack that drowns out the noise of spiraling thoughts. Let His truth be the place your mind returns to over and over.

And here's what I want you to know: you're not expected to do it perfectly. God isn't measuring your performance. He's simply inviting you into His presence, and all you have to do is say yes.

This journey isn't a straight line. Some days you'll feel strong, and other days fear will flood in out of nowhere. But that doesn't mean you're doing it wrong.

I'm seven years out, and I still have moments when fear catches me off guard—when my mind races and those old thoughts start to creep back in. I don't beat myself up for having them, and neither should you.

I've learned where to take those fears, how to reframe them, and what truths to replace them with. And the most important part: Take them straight to Jesus. Let His truth anchor you—again, and again, and again.

Truth to Anchor You

> "The weapons we fight with are not the weapons of the world. On the contrary, they have divine power to demolish strongholds. We demolish arguments and every pretension that sets itself up against the knowledge of God, and we take captive every thought to make it obedient to Christ."
> (2 Corinthians 10:4-5 NIV)

When fear visits, remember this: you are not powerless. You don't have to entertain every thought that knocks on the door of your mind. God has equipped you with divine power—not just to survive the fear, but to demolish the strongholds it tries to build.

Every time you pause, reframe, and replace fear with truth, you're actively exercising the power God has given you. In those moments, you are choosing peace. You are choosing life.

This is our model: we don't fight fear with logic or willpower, because those can only take us so far. We fight it with the truth found in God's Word—the only thing that has the power to transform our minds and hearts.

The more you speak God's truth, the more you saturate your mind with it, the more peace will naturally replace the fear that once tried to take up residence in your heart. Start small. One verse at a time. One prayer at a time. Write them. Speak them. Repeat them until they are louder than your fear.

God's Word isn't just available for knowledge. It's available for power. Use it, my friend, to replace those fearful thoughts that sneak in.

Final Thoughts

I never got my MRI doorway.

What I got instead was a slow, quiet realization that fear might never completely go away—and that's okay. It's not brokenness. It's not failure. It's just part of surviving cancer.

Fear still whispers to me sometimes, louder than I want it to. But I've learned it doesn't get to run the show. It doesn't get to decide how I show up in my life or how I embrace each day. I've chosen not to let fear steal my joy. And you can make that same choice.

If you've been feeling afraid, even now, even after the good reports, I just want you to know: me too. I get it. It's okay to feel caught in that strange, in-between space where you're both grateful and nervous, hopeful and holding your breath.

And if that tension has made you feel like you're doing survivorship "wrong," please hear me when I say: you're not.

Fear doesn't mean you don't trust God. It doesn't cancel out your gratitude. It just means you're human. A human who's been through a lot.

I hope you're feeling a little relief right now, just knowing you're not the only one who's ever felt this way. That maybe you're not as alone in this as you thought.

And when fear shows up next time—and it probably will—you don't have to panic. Just pause. Breathe. Go back to what's true. You already have what you need to face it. You've already come this far.

Now that you've exhaled a little and maybe even wiped a few tears, it's time to take the next step. Because while we can't always stop fear from showing up, we can be ready for it. I want to share some of the tools that have helped me the most. Simple, powerful things you can return to anytime fear starts to rise.

Not theory. Not fluff. Just real tools for real life after cancer.

Next Steps: Practical Strategies, Prompts, and Prayer

The following tip will help you build on the teachings of normalizing, reframing, and replacing fear. By putting them into practice, you'll strengthen your ability to walk in peace and trust God's promises, no matter what.

Practical Strategies to Reframe Fear

- **Name It** – Acknowledge when fear shows up. Don't dismiss it—identify it. Sometimes just saying "I'm afraid right now" lessens its grip.

- **Write It Down** – Journaling your fears helps disarm their power and lets you invite God into them.
- **Speak God's Word Out Loud** – Scripture is a weapon. Verses like Isaiah 41:10, Psalm 23, and 2 Timothy 1:7 remind your heart who's in charge.
- **Reach Out** – Don't walk through the fear alone. Find someone safe, another survivor, a counselor, a friend who "gets it."
- **Choose Gratitude** – Gratitude doesn't erase fear, but it does shift your perspective. Even the smallest joys—sunlight on your skin, a good laugh—anchor you to the present.

Journaling Prompts

- "What am I afraid of right now, and how does it compare to God's promises in my life?"
- "How has God carried me before, and how can I trust Him to carry me again?"
- "What verse or truth will anchor me when fear returns?"

Tangible Ways to Take Charge of How You Navigate Your Post-Cancer Journey

- **Create a Comfort Routine for Scan Days**: Make a playlist of calming songs, wear your favorite cozy socks, or plan something enjoyable after your appointment.
- **Write a Letter to Yourself**: Reflect on how far you've come, acknowledge your fears, and celebrate your

strength. Read this letter before an appointment and/or as you wait on results.

- **Find a Safe Space to Talk**: Join a survivor support group, seek therapy, or talk to someone who's walked this road before.

- **Create a "Truth Bank"**: Write down 3-5 verses to speak over yourself before appointments. Choose to view fear through the lens of Scripture.

- **Pack Your Bag**: Choose a fun bag you already own or consider purchasing a new one. Fill it with all things comfort: Scripture, prayer cards to remind you of God's promises, a favorite pen and journal, a book you enjoy reading, healthy snacks, fuzzy socks, a blanket or shawl. No rules on this one. This is your go-to bag for any cancer-related appointment. Grab and go.

- **Commit to Take Care of You:** Explore the choices you can make to support your overall health and help minimize the risk of cancer recurrence. Prioritize nutrition choices, skincare free of harmful chemicals, and commit to staying active in ways that support your strength and vitality.

Prayer

Lord,

You see my heart, and You know the fear that still sneaks in, uninvited and unwanted. Thank You for reminding me that fear doesn't disqualify my faith; it just gives me another reason to run to You. Help me to trust You when my mind spirals and my body remembers. Anchor me in Your truth, and teach me how to carry fear without letting it carry me away. Thank You for the gift of time—and the gift of today. Amen.

The next time fear whispers, meet it with truth. You are held. You are not alone. And your story is still being written—by the One who never lets go.

Chapter 3

Trust Your Gut and the Holy Spirit

By Page Jeske

> "THE LORD'S RIGHT HAND HAS DONE MIGHTY THINGS! I WILL NOT DIE BUT LIVE, AND WILL PROCLAIM WHAT THE LORD HAS DONE." PSALM 118:16-17 (NIV)

I had not been feeling well for a couple of months. The extreme tiredness was not normal for me, and I had noticed that my tummy was bloated. Despite feeling tired, I had been exercising a lot that summer as I continued to train for my first 100-mile road-biking race. A century ride.

After my fifty-first birthday, I realized I should have had a colonoscopy a year before on my fiftieth birthday, according to health screening recommendations. Turning fifty the year before had been traumatic enough, so I had put off having my screening done.

As 2016 began to wind down, I thought I'd better go ahead and get my colonoscopy done. My gut was trying to tell me something. So I needed to trust that feeling. I felt prompted by the Holy Spirit to get this done, and besides, my insurance deductible was about to be met. This needed to happen prior to December 31st.

The soonest that I could get in was December 21. I followed the liquid, clear broth, Jell-O diet a couple of days before the procedure, and then drank the concoction that is part of the screening prep the night before the procedure.

Taking the day off work, I had arranged for a dear friend, Lawnie Kay, to be my designated driver to and from the colonoscopy.

At the hospital, I was given propofol, the anesthetic that they call the Michael Jackson drug, which knocks you out for the procedure. I knew a lot of the nurses who worked in Dr. Ward's office from when I was the injury prevention coordinator in the hospital for nine years.

One of the nurses greeted me and explained how the procedure would go. I tried to relax and told myself that this was just a screening and it would all be fine. Another nurse came in and hooked up my IV, and I was quickly asleep. They are not kidding when they tell you it is "the best nap of a lifetime."

I woke up in recovery, and a nurse let me know that Dr. Ward would be in shortly to go over the results of the screening.

Dr. Ward came into the room and closed the door behind him. "I am so glad you came in for your screening," he said.

"I know, me too, glad that is off my list. Now I can focus on the rest of my Christmas preparations."

"No, I don't think you understand. I am really glad that you came in. We found a mass," Dr Ward said in a steady, yet concerned tone."

"Oh really? What do you mean by that—a polyp?" I said.

"Actually, no. We found a mass that looks to be about five centimeters in circumference." He paused just slightly, then said, "It's cancer. You will need to have a CT scan as soon as possible to see if it has spread outside of the colon wall."

I was stunned and did not know what to say. The word cancer hit me like a freight train. After everything else I had gone through—abandonment, divorce, and a horrible car accident where I had to learn to walk again. And now cancer?

Dr. Ward then showed me a color picture of the inside of my colon. I could clearly see the mass. He said, "The mass is in the cecum area of your colon. You will most likely need to have surgery soon to remove the cancer and that section of your colon." As I looked at the picture, it all became too real. This was my body. I had cancer.

It felt as if all the alarm systems in my body were on high alert, but I tried to take a deep breath and absorb everything the doctor was saying. I looked up at Lawnie Kay, and she, too, looked concerned and worried.

"If at all possible, I'd like to have the CT done today since I've taken the day off from work and I am already here," I told Dr. Ward.

"I'll see if they can fit you in right away," he said and left the room.

God, in his goodness and graciousness, had one of my friends, Mindy, running the radiology schedule that day.

So when Dr. Ward called down there, she moved patients around on the schedule like pieces on a crowded chessboard to make sure they could get me in immediately.

Once I was cleared to be transported to radiology, they whisked me down to CT for the prep and the test. After the CT scan, I was released to go home. "Try not to worry," the nurse said. Dr. Ward will call you with the results of the tests as soon as he gets them, probably later this afternoon."

What they were trying to rule out was if the cancer had spread to my lungs, kidneys, or other organs.

I went home and tried to rest and cast all my anxiety on the Lord. About 3:00 pm that day, Dr. Ward called. "Page, the CT shows the mass has **not** spread outside of the colon or to the liver or kidneys. We will know about the lymph nodes once we do the surgery."

I was so relieved to hear this news. It was a bright spot in what had felt like a very dark and gloomy day.

Dr. Ward told me that he was going to refer me to Dr. Blair, the chief surgeon, so that surgery could be scheduled as soon as possible.

As I hung up the phone, a sense of gratefulness seemed to flood my body. The cancer had not spread outside the colon wall to other organs. But I also thought about all the unknowns ahead. Until the surgery was performed, I couldn't really know the outcome.

The next day at work, I tried to act as normally as possible. I called my boss, Desi, to let her know what was going on and that I would need to make arrangements to take time off for the surgery and recuperation. Desi was incredibly understanding and told me not to worry about work and that she would be praying for me.

Prior to the diagnosis, I had planned to take a week of vacation after Christmas, but had not made plans to go anywhere. Even then, the Lord had been leading me in arranging my vacation days.

My boys were with their Dad for the Christmas break, so I was alone to process this trial and give it all to the Lord. I had told them about the findings and the upcoming surgery, and I would see them after Christmas.

I spent Christmas Eve dinner with my dear friend Michelle and her family, and we attended the Christmas Eve service at our church together. During the service, I was so glad to be surrounded by the songs of hope and joy as we celebrated the night before the birth of our Savior.

I awoke Christmas morning to a thick blanket of snow on the ground, a beautiful way to begin Christmas day. I slept in a little and then prepped the food that I was taking to my friend Doris' home for Christmas dinner. She had graciously invited me to come and share Christmas with her family so that I would not be alone.

We had a wonderful time eating and enjoying each other and the beautiful day. Her daughter Jessica was there. She was an oncology nurse in Boise. So I shared my pictures and the report from Dr. Ward about my colon cancer. I was able to ask a lot of questions, and she helped answer many of them. I also expressed my concerns and fears about the cancer and the upcoming surgery. When I got home that night, I told the Lord how GOOD He had been to provide someone for me to talk with and answer my questions. Once again, the goodness of the Lord and His provision along the way.

On Tuesday, December 27, I had a follow-up appointment with Dr. Ward, and he went over the CT results with me in person. And confirmed that Dr. Blair, the chief of surgery with a specialty in laparoscopic surgery, would be the one doing the surgery.

My pre op appointment with Dr. Blair was on December 28th. My friend Shelly, who was a nurse and had been a previous patient of Dr. Blair's, agreed to go to this appointment with me. She helped me think through questions to ask, and we prayed together before my appointment with him.

Dr. Blair explained that I would be having a colectomy. This involved cutting a portion of my colon out and possibly some of my large intestine. He would connect sections of my colon to make it function well again. They hoped to get all the cancer by removing that section of my colon and the tumor. While in the surgery, they would extract about twelve or more lymph nodes for testing as well. Then they would send off the lymph nodes to be tested to see if they were at all cancerous.

I let Dr. Blair know that I was a single mom and was worried about missing a lot of work, and for insurance purposes, it would be best if the surgery could transpire before the end of the year. Dr. Blair seemed to understand my predicament. He explained how I would need to prepare for surgery, and then we followed him out to the scheduling and receptionist's desk.

"How would December 30th at 7:30 am work for you?" he said.

"That is great. Absolutely, the sooner the better, thank you." I replied.

Shelley and I agreed that she would accompany me on the day of my surgery. I needed someone to take me to the hospital and to communicate with my family back east and my boys about how I was doing. I was so thankful for her willingness to do this for me during her Christmas break. I did not want to put my twenty-year-old son in that position, especially if something were to go awry.

On Friday, December 30, Shelley picked me up to take me to the hospital for the surgery. She and I prayed together before I went into surgery, and it felt so good to commit all of this to the Lord.

After waking up from surgery, I was a bit groggy and sore. A nurse wheeled me from recovery to my room on the second floor. I was told that the stapled incision above my belly button was only about two inches in length. Shelley was there to greet me. She had brought me a beautiful Christmas-motif hand-stitched quilt in reds and greens, and grays that was just the perfect size for a twin bed. She said her mother-in-law, Carla, had sent it to me and wanted me to use this in the hospital to make it a bit more like home.

Alone in my room, I ran my hand over the bright Christmas quilt that made my sterile hospital room, my home for a few days, feel more like a decorated room in a cozy retreat center. I felt so grateful and so cared for by that beautiful gesture. As I looked down at the quilt, I thanked God for all the many ways that He had seen me through some difficult days.

In the stillness of the moment, I sensed He was saying, "Don't worry, Page. Don't you see I have you covered?" It was as if He was reminding me of how He had covered me in His love and the love of His people.

The next day, I was starting to feel a little bit better, and I could walk around some.

Then Dr. Blair came by on his rounds to give me an update on how the surgery had gone, he said, "I took out ten inches of your colon, and the mass, as well as two inches of your intestine. And also your appendix because it was inflamed and very diseased."

As I was absorbing that, he reassured me, saying, "The cancer was stage 2A. It had not metastasized. It appears we got all of it." He went on to say that he had also biopsied seventeen lymph nodes. And that we needed to wait for the results to come back from pathology.

Feeling good about what my surgeon was telling me, I said, "The surgery was not that bad. I already feel much better."

Dr Blair then replied kindly, "Well, how you feel and heal is largely based on your attitude, and you have had a great attitude through all of this." These were such kind words that he shared with me.

We were coming up on New Year's Eve, and I was so grateful. I had a lot to be thankful for. The surgery had been done before the end of the year, so my medical deductible could be met.

Those days in the hospital felt like a four-day church service. Christian friends and pastors came to see me and prayed for me for complete healing. There was a steady stream of friends who brought gifts and flowers to cheer me up in the hospital. And as my boys visited me each day, I was grateful that they got to experience how God's people were living out being Jesus in the flesh.

Monday morning came, and I had to make sure my blood levels and all systems were working so that I could be discharged. After lunch that day, I got the word that I could go home. I called my boys, David and Champ, and they came to get me. They helped transport me, my belongings, and all the flowers and gifts. I was so ready to be home and to see my sweet little dog, Ginger—a shih tzu/poodle mix.

That whole week, we had a huge snowfall in the Magic Valley, Twin Falls, where we lived. There was a record number of inches and the coldest temperatures since the 1980s. The boys were great about shoveling the snow while I rested and regained my strength.

A small group of friends brought meals to the house. My sons loved that dose of homemade goodness. The last thing I wanted to do was stand up for long periods of time or cook. So all the meals were an answer to prayer. And my boys got to see the hands and feet of Jesus once again.

Waiting for the test results from the biopsies of my lymph nodes was hard. We got another dump of snow, so much so that the doctors' offices were closed for a couple of days. By the end of the week, I still did not know the results from the biopsies. I prayed and prayed that I would hear from my doctor on that Friday and not have to wait over the weekend to get the news.

Early Friday afternoon, Dr. Blair called. Finally, I was going to get an answer. "So I have the results from your lymph node biopsies, and I am happy to report they came back clear. They are NOT cancerous."

A deep joy and silent shout of Hallelujah welled up inside me as he spoke.

"So that means that the cancer has not spread? You got all of it in the surgery?" My voice must have sounded a bit tentative. I think my doctor sensed a bit of doubt in my voice and my need for more clarification.

"Exactly, you will not have to undergo any chemotherapy for radiation at all." Dr Blair replied.

I was absolutely relieved and thankful. "This is great news, Dr. Blair, thank you for clarifying," I responded on the phone.

Dr. Blair said that I would need to have a baseline CT of my lungs to make sure that there were no spots on my lungs.

They had recommended taking two to four weeks off work after the surgery that I had had. However, I went back on January 9th, fewer than ten days post-surgery. Again, I was a single Mom, and if I did not work, I did not get paid, so I went back to work full days instead of partial days.

On January 12th, Dr. Blair took my staples out of my abdomen. And I was so glad to have them gone.

On January 19th, I went to see Dr. Manning, my oncologist, for the first time. As I approached the hospital and saw the words, Mountain States Tumor Institute (MSTI) above the automatic doors, I thought, This is one door I never imagined I'd be going through.

Dr. Manning let me know that my "new normal" was to come to do blood draws at MSTI every three months to monitor any rise in my numbers. For colon cancer, you want CEA (carcinoembryonic antigen) levels to be less than or equal to three nanograms per milliliter. CEA is a tumor marker for colon cancer. When it starts going up, it can be an indication of cancer in the body. My CT lung scan was right after my appointment with Dr. Manning.

The radiology tech informed me after the CT of my lungs was done that someone would call me the next day with the results.

The next day at work, I got a call with the result of my lung CT. It was negative. I was completely clear of cancer! I would not have to undergo chemo or radiation, hair loss, and other side effects. It had been exactly thirty-three days from diagnosis to the news that I was cancer-free. The time seemed much longer than that. That afternoon, I left work light and full of joy, and so grateful for the Lord's healing.

Isaiah 58:8-9 (NIV), "Then your light will break forth like the dawn, and your healing will quickly appear; then your righteousness will go before you, and the glory of the Lord will be your rear guard. Then you will call, and the Lord will answer; you will call for help, and he will say, here am I."

Once I had regained my strength, a couple of months after my cancer surgery, I began retraining for my first 100-mile Century ride. I was determined to do a century in June of that year. After registering online, I recruited some bike sisters to go with me to Utah and compete in my first century ride, the Little Red. In 2016, I had done the 50-miler on this same course, but this would be my first 100-miler.

So on June 2, 2017, in Logan, Utah, just six months after my colon cancer surgery, I finished my first 100-mile bike ride. My first Century ride. Then, three weeks later, I finished my second century, the MS Harmon bike ride in the same area of Utah.

Then on July 22, I completed eighty-five miles of the Cycle Magic Valley bike ride in Twin Falls, ID.

On my birthday that year, I rode fifty-two miles to celebrate my health and healing. God had given me more life to live and I wanted to live it to the fullest.

Now at 59, I am still cancer-free, and so grateful for each day the Lord has given me.

In the aftermath of my cancer surgery, I am passionate about using my voice and words to educate others about screenings as a colon cancer awareness spokesperson here in my community.

As a living example, I have been interviewed on TV, and my local hospital featured me in an article. I have spoken at a cancer fundraiser and been a speaker at our local community college in some health classes, addressing the importance of screenings.

There are a couple of things that I have learned through my cancer journey that I would like to share with you. And prayerfully, these will be helpful teaching points.

1. Listen to your gut and the Holy Spirit.

"But the Helper, the Holy Spirit whom the Father will send in my name, *he will teach you all things* and bring to remembrance all that I have said to you." (John 14:26, NKJV, emphasis added)

Because I was in tune with my body while training for the 100-mile bike ride, I was able to discern that I was tired and my energy was not what it had normally been. I also noticed the bloating in my abdominal area, another symptom of something being wrong. I later learned that the overtiredness was due to the fact that I was anemic because I was gradually losing blood in my stool due to the colon cancer. And as I prayed about it, the Holy Spirit was the one who prompted me to get a colonoscopy scheduled on December 21st that year. I would never have done this at that time of year had the spirit's prompting not been so strong.

Another verse that is so encouraging about the power of the Holy Spirit is one in Romans.

"In the same way, the Spirit helps us in our weakness. We do not know what we ought to pray for, but the Spirit himself intercedes for us through wordless groans. And he who searches our hearts knows the mind of the Spirit, because the Spirit intercedes for God's people in accordance with the will of God." (Romans 8:26-27 NIV)

2. **The body of Christ and the community are a powerful way that the Lord can minister to us here on earth. Allow people to serve you.**

Allow your friends and family to do things for you, and help you if you are going through a difficult time, recovering from a cancer surgery, or just healing.

"Each of you should use whatever gift you have received to serve others, as faithful stewards of God's grace in its various forms. If anyone speaks, they should do so as one who speaks the very words of God. If anyone serves, they should do so with the strength God provides, so that in all things God may be praised through Jesus Christ. To Him be the glory and the power forever and ever, Amen." (1 Peter 4:10-11, NIV)

As I mentioned in my story, Lawnie Kay and Shelly took me to appointments and surgeries. And prayed for me before my procedures. Many friends and folks from my church visited me in the hospital, which made that four-day-long stay go much more quickly. People brought delicious meals to my house for days after my surgery. And as I healed, that made eating and feeding my boys so much easier for me while they were home for Christmas break. And my sons got to see the hands and feet of Jesus ministering to our family.

Accept the cards, the flowers, the meals, and the rides to follow-up appointments. Allow the body of Christ to work and be used as the Lord intended for it to work.

One of my friends, Staci, and her Mom, Barbara, came and took down all my Christmas decorations and put them away in my garage. That was something I absolutely could not have done because of all the stretching and moving those tasks required. I had abdominal stitches, so that was not something I could have taken on. They also picked up some yummy soup from one of my favorite restaurants and brought that over for us to enjoy while they put away Christmas.

3. **Testify to others about the way that the Lord has worked in your healing journey. Allow your valleys and pain to be the places where others see the goodness of the Lord and His powerful healing hands.**

"Praise the Lord, my soul, and forget not all His benefits—who forgives all your sins and *heals all your diseases.*" (Psalm 103:2-3, NIV, emphasis added)

I know that my story is unique. The surgery was able to get all the cancer, and it had not spread anywhere else. So I did not have to have radiation or any chemotherapy at all. And God was very gracious and thorough in healing my body. And as I am writing this, almost 8 years post-surgery, I am still cancer-free. My first colonoscopy at age 51 literally saved my life. Preventative screening is so important.

I honestly cannot express my gratefulness to the Lord for how He chose to heal me. I know that things could have turned out so differently and not in the positive way that they did. So I am very vocal about my healing and what the Lord did. It is important to me to share with others how God healed me and to testify to His goodness and mercy.

"Even when I am old and gray, do not forsake me, my God, *till I declare your power to the next generation, your mighty acts to all who are to come.*" (Psalm 71:18, NIV, emphasis added)

"*My tongue will tell of your righteous acts all day long* for those who wanted to harm me have been put to shame and confusion." (Psalm 71:24, NIV, emphasis added)

As a living example, I have been interviewed on TV, and my local hospital featured me in an article. I have spoken at a cancer fundraiser and been a speaker at our local community college in some health classes, addressing the importance of screenings.

It has been my joy to write this chapter during March, Colon Cancer Awareness month. And being a part of this book was an answer to prayer. I had prayed for an opportunity to share my story with more people during this important month, and God allowed this opportunity to write for Hopewriters. So once again, I am so very thankful for my life, and I will continue to testify of his goodness for generations to come.

Prayer

Lord Jesus, I pray for the readers right now. Whatever they are going through at this time, that you might use the words of this chapter and your holy scriptures to minister and speak in powerful ways. Thank you for our difficult times, valleys, and illnesses that allow us to lean even more on you, and through them, we become more like you. Help us to be a reflection of you to those who are around us. May we be an example of Christ to all who are watching. And most importantly, may you draw them to yourselves. Thank you for being a good, good Father. Please speak personally and profoundly to each reader who picks up this book. May they be forever changed because of you and who you are. And we ask all of this in the powerful and holy name of Jesus.

Chapter 4

God's Grace in the Waiting: Faith Refined Through Suffering

By Amy McClain

"YOU WERE TIRED OUT BY THE LENGTH OF YOUR ROAD,
YET YOU DID NOT SAY, 'IT IS HOPELESS.'
YOU FOUND RENEWED STRENGTH,
THEREFORE, YOU DID NOT FAINT."
ISAIAH 57:10 (NASB)

---

*B*e careful what you wish for. There was a time when I complained in my heart that my life had been too easy.

I had been blessed with an idyllic childhood, having grown up in a close-knit, loving family. Up to this point in my life, I had never experienced anything really difficult or distressing. As a young believer and a college student, I was devouring stories of saints undergoing tremendous trials and testing that both informed their faith as well as created resilient, stalwart lives to emulate. I wondered how I could grow as a Christian and live as an example to others if my faith had never truly been proven.

My college days were full of strenuous studies and exhilarating experiences, including a study-abroad semester living in a thatched hut on the arid grasslands of Kenya. I was there to research the effects of environmental and cultural change on the country's iconic wildlife, but my narrow American worldview was irreversibly altered when I visited a Maasai tribal village and met an eleven-year-old child bride who had been abused and treated as chattel. Firsthand, I witnessed the positive societal change that occurred when a compassionate missionary family living in the village taught them to exchange their evil practices with repentance, grace, and God's forgiveness. Running in the African heat one day, I scanned the cloudless blue expanse overhead and opened my heart to being used by the Lord in tribal missions. Soon after that, I received a surprise love letter in the mail from the boy back home who had already captured my heart. He, too, had a similar desire to be used by God to spread His love where it had not been known. Our destinies were united by marriage in a simple wedding ceremony, the day after our college graduations.

After college, God called my new husband and me to a missionary career serving one of the least-reached populations on planet Earth. These remote tribes of the dense Papuan rainforests were cut off from any gospel witness by their extremely remote environment, hostile culture, and linguistic isolation. If no one had set foot into their world, they would have remained just as ignorant of God's love for them as they had been for millennia. So in 2005, my husband

and I responded to the need, moving overseas with our three very young children to study the Indonesian language on the highly populated island of Java. After completing almost two years of language school, we moved a thousand miles eastward across the Indonesian archipelago of tropical islands to the wild province of Papua. We found the stone-age cultures there to be in stark contrast to the polite and refined Javanese; the hundreds of unwritten tribal languages, a new linguistic mystery to unravel.

It was two more years of intense survey work before our family (now seven of us) and the rest of our missionary team would finally choose a small village in a clearing in the vast rainforest where we were given permission to build our home. With no roads inland, our location was only accessible on foot or by helicopter, so the move-in process was slowed down by limited cargo space and the occasional sling-load. In 2009, we began the arduous task of learning an unwritten language, deciphering its complicated grammar structure, and encoding its phonemes into an alphabet. In the beginning, it was humbling to be so ignorant of these people's unintelligible words and foreign ways, but the language learning process took more than six years before my husband was fluent enough to begin to translate the Bible. Our team hoped to eventually earn the right to share with our friends the Good News of Jesus Christ's salvation for their souls.

Our growing family loved the adventure of dwelling in a rainforest. What we gave up in familiar comforts, we traded for a life that was never dull. We gleaned vital knowledge from our nomadic hunter-gatherer friends about living off the land. Bananas, papayas, guavas, pineapples, starfruit, red fruit, jackfruit, and mango grew like weeds in our yard, and our neighbors were skilled at hunting wild boar and deer, which they eagerly sold to us. We were surprised that while impoverished in many other ways, they had meat in abundance! Gardening was a more difficult prospect, as our high hopes to grow our own vegetables were smothered by the rotting jungle mud and eaten by trillions of devouring insects. As I daily homeschooled my five children, I found the educational opportunities in our surroundings to be one of a kind! Science was one of our favorite subjects, as we lived in one of the most biologically diverse ecosystems on the planet. All five of the kids became zookeepers-in-training as they cared for a menagerie of orphaned wild animals: baby tree kangaroos, cuscuses, cockatoos, parrots, bandicoots, wallabies, frilled lizards, and cassowaries.

As a native New Yorker, it was a completely otherworldly experience for me to be living as part of an indigenous community that depended on one another for survival. Yet God gave me such compassion for my village friends that I did not want to be anywhere else. Over time, we earned their trust and were addressed by the same endearing kinship terms they used with one another: I was *kaiyai* (mother), *mbelian* (younger sibling), or *pepai* (older sister) to them. Though I had come from a foreign world, living among them enabled me to identify with the same harsh realities they faced: days full of mundane tasks in the equatorial heat, caring for my family's endless needs, and more often than not, facing serious illness as a normal part of life. We discovered a nemesis in the ever-present mosquito, as our lowland location was subject to the dreaded mosquito-borne parasites that cause malaria, dengue fever, and filariasis (which causes the grotesque condition known as elephantiasis). Giardia, amoeba, typhoid abounded; even tuberculosis was always lurking. With rudimentary medical skills, we treated what ailments we could and arranged helicopter medivacs to a coastal hospital for the life-threatening emergencies. While I welcomed the challenges of living in the village, I was also becoming chronically fatigued, and found myself sick with malaria so often that we started joking that "being ill was my ministry." So, I was no stranger to serious illness when cancer came along. I just wasn't prepared for how it would interrupt the carefully laid plans I had for my life.

Over the first thirteen years of our overseas missionary career, we had experienced many health setbacks requiring emergency evacuations and medical furloughs. These were all disorienting and disrupting, but each time we recovered, we would get to return to the little corner of the world we called home in Papua. When we were healthy, the ministry work was moving along well, with the first Scripture portions and Bible teaching material having been translated into the tribal language. Ministry motivation and momentum were at an all-time high in early 2018.

Then, we planned a brief trip back to the U.S. during the summer months to settle our first homeschool graduate into college. We traversed the country, reporting what God was doing through our ministry to partners and supporting churches, eager to quickly return and get back to work. But this time, the brief few months turned into several agonizing years, as shock waves of disruption barred our way—unwanted interruptions and hard stops, family health struggles and hospitalizations, team disunity and financial strain—these, among other issues, prevented us from returning to our field of service as planned. Even larger life crises were waiting, as yet unknown to us, behind the scenes.

Yet, when our family seemed well enough to travel again, we tried again and again to get back to our jungle home and friends. One year, we had purchased seven return plane tickets and applied for another entrance visa, but this time, the worldwide coronavirus pandemic shut down the international borders. And once again, we had to remain in our passport country, which no longer felt like home. In many ways, staying put was harder than going in the first place. We longed for an open door to continue the exhausting but worthwhile work that we were doing there. The fact that our tribe was still waiting to hear the entire message of God's Word clearly taught in their own language continually tugged at my heart. So many of them were sick and even dying before we had the chance to teach them the Good News. Why, when we were so willing to answer His call, would God keep closing this door? We knew God was ultimately in charge, but our hearts still questioned ....

Then in July of 2020, at a routine annual physical, a doctor in residency performed my physical exam 'by the book', starting at the top of my cranium and palpating every inch down to my big toe. She quickly found a nodule in my neck that I would need to have biopsied. I am grateful for her thorough examination, or I may not have known about the tumor that had likely been slowly growing inside me for more than a decade. It took three doctors to definitively diagnose it. The first one was sure that it was cancer just by looking at the ultrasound, and he announced this to me even before he performed a biopsy.

I was shocked–the word *cancer* dropped heavy in the room like a ton of bricks. An uninvited intruder that I couldn't ignore but had to face. The doctor assured me it was treatable. But still, *cancer*.

Alone at this appointment, I made my way to my car in a daze and called my husband in tears. He helped ease my fears by saying that we needed a second opinion. The second doctor didn't think it was cancer, but autoimmune thyroid disease instead. He did, however, perform another biopsy. Later, I received confounding results: 1st biopsy–negative for cancer, 2nd biopsy–positive! Even worse, this second biopsy was positive for thyroid cancer in a lymph node, which meant that it had already spread beyond the thyroid bed. It had the daunting name of *metastatic papillary thyroid carcinoma*. Needless to say, I was confused and scared.

Seeking support from our spiritual community was just as important to us as the medical advice, so we asked our church elders to pray for our clarity and decisions about treatment, as well as physical healing. Soon, we received a call from one of our elders who said, "I saw your prayer request. I know a doctor who can help you. He happens to also be a believer." As it turned out, God had handpicked a highly skilled head and neck surgeon from a nearby prestigious university hospital. He saw more lymph nodes on the ultrasound that he wanted to biopsy during surgery, and he had the exacting skill and experience needed to painstakingly scrape cancerous lymph nodes off vital structures in my neck, including the carotid artery. By the end of the invasive surgical and radiation treatments, I was minus a thyroid and about a dozen cancerous lymph nodes scattered throughout my neck. In exact, but scary medical terms, I had endured a double-lobed thyroidectomy, lymphadenectomy, radical neck dissection, and radioactive iodine therapy. There were days I felt like some fictional character out of the recesses of a classical novel (not unlike Frankenstein, with a six-inch incision across my neck) or from a futuristic science-fiction tale (when a Geiger counter placed near my radioactive body literally beeped incessantly)!

My recovery and adjustment to aggressive thyroid hormone therapy were painstakingly slow. Friends and family rallied, cheering me and my household on towards healing. Amazing sacrifices on my behalf were made during those months in the fall of 2020. Despite the prevailing shelter-in-place orders of those days, so many reached out beyond their comfort zones to offer support and care. My elderly parents and only sister collaborated to continue the homeschooling of my children without interruption. My newly widowed mother-in-law also moved into our home to offer help. Though COVID restrictions had kept me from having visitors in the hospital, after two sterile but lonely days in recovery, I returned from the hospital to a full home and the joyful cacophony of family. My bedroom walls, brightly plastered with construction paper cut-outs of happy face emojis and hand-drawn posters crafted by my entire family, caused my eyes to brim with tears as I read their words of encouragement: "With God ... you can overcome anything!" Our church family brought over nutritious meals that fed us all for several weeks. The beautiful cards and flowers overflowing on my bedside table even eclipsed the multitudes of medication bottles, as a reminder that I was surrounded with tremendous love and support in the midst of this trial. I enjoyed the surprise of thoughtful care packages that came in the mail. One day, an old college friend called to reconnect and had me laughing so hard I thought my neck stitches would fall out! Yet that laughter was a gift that I would not quickly forget.

During the week or so after my radioactive iodine therapy, I had to be physically isolated from anyone in or nearing their childbearing years, including my husband and children, since my body would continue to emit possibly harmful radioactivity. As a natural introvert, I craved this alone time and retreated happily to my bedroom and books. Reading the Bible became as integral to me as my daily sustenance. My mind, body, and spirit felt strengthened with the declarations of hope found on each page I turned:

"This is my comfort in my affliction, that Thy word has revived me." (Psalm 119:50, NASB)

I found more time for meditating on passages that fed my soul. Psalm 73 had always been near and dear to my heart. Verse 28 called to me:

"But as for me, the nearness of God is my good; I have made the Lord God my refuge, that I may tell of all Thy works." (Psalm 73:28, NASB)

Like the Psalmist, I was comforted by the fact that I could draw near and be held, quiet my worries and fears, and know that my cries for help were heard.

I was determined that this life interruption wouldn't be wasted. If God deemed it important enough to put off the eternal work we were doing overseas, then he must want me to learn something lasting from it. *Perhaps there was eternal work to be done in my heart?*

The question of God's goodness was ever before me: Did He care? Was this really His best for me? How did cancer fit into my urgent plan to bring His Good News to the ends of the earth? Early on during my cancer treatment, I wrote this plea to God in my journal:

> *"Do I look at my circumstances through the grid of God's character, or do I judge God's character through the grid of my circumstances? This has been my problem. My eyes have been off the prize—and my anxieties are fueled by what feels terrible about these circumstances. Somewhere in the midst of this cancer, may You somehow bring some healing to the deeper issues of my heart?"*

It was not only physical healing I so desperately needed but also deliverance from the disappointment in God's current will for my life that threatened my spiritual and emotional health. It was my prayer to stay near to God's heart, even though I lamented the pain and struggle. He was indeed bringing my faith through the refining fires that my much younger self had ignorantly asked for all those years before.

The question in my heart was not whether God Himself was good. I believed He was infinitely good beyond my comprehension. The God who gave up His Only Son, Jesus, unto death for me, so that I could be forgiven of my sins and be reconciled with Him, was a good, good God indeed. There is no other god like Him. In whom else would I place my trust?

Instead, it was a matter of doubting His will for *my* life. Would I fully believe that His plan *for me* was good? My trust in God's goodness could not hang simply on pat "Sunday school" answers, but it had to be grounded on the truth of His Word and on the hard evidence of His good hand in my life in the past. What did the Scriptures tell me?

"'For I know the plans I have for you,' says the Lord. 'They are plans for good and not disaster, to give you a future and a hope.'" (Jeremiah 29:11, NLT)

Certainly, looking back on my life, I could see that my God had always been faithful. His presence with me was a constant, whether I was fearful and needy or overwhelmed with blessings. Those blessings were easy to count: my caring husband, five beautiful children, numerous family members, and friends who all gave sacrificially to be there for us in our time of need. The "coincidence" that God brought us home to the States at this very time—so I could have access to the diagnosis and medical treatment my cancer required—was not an accident, but rather a God-ordained blessing. Over the years, He had proven Himself as our faithful Provider, especially at times when we felt utterly dependent on Him, like when we were all suffering from malarial fevers in the middle of the jungle. The fact that God allowed us to suffer did not please Him. No, He was not rejoicing in our trials, but certainly lamenting along with us the fact that sin has had such dire consequences upon this broken world. I recognized cancer as one tangible evidence of the effects of that universal brokenness on our bodies. I believed that He did not choose it for me just to watch me fight it alone, but He promised to be yoked with me, bearing the pain of every heart-wrenching moment in the battle. That greater knowledge of His faithful presence with me would ultimately strengthen my faith, and not just for my own good, but to benefit others who were weary from the length of their own journey.

The verse I chose for the beginning of this chapter, Isaiah 57:10, appears to be a comfort to all of us who find ourselves weary and tired out from the unrelenting difficulty of the path laid out before us. Have you, too, felt that your road is unbearably long? The end may be out of sight, and the pain along the way seems more than one can endure. Any exhortation to 'journey on' just seems cruel; *"If only they knew how hard this is for me,"* we contend. I can certainly relate to that, needing to find some small hope to cling to, a source of strength to continue putting one foot in front of the other. At first, reading this verse, I seemed to think it meant that God would help me recover the strength to go on (which, of course, is true as evidenced elsewhere in the Bible). But upon studying the surrounding verses in their context, I discovered that what Isaiah is actually alluding to here is almost the very opposite. The prophet is rebuking Israel for their self-sufficiency, for being wise in their own eyes and continuing stubbornly in their sinful ways instead of repenting and returning to God. Here he was addressing their self-propelled persistence and rejection of God's grace and help. This was a different interpretation altogether. When reading Scripture, we must always ask ourselves what the original intent of the passage meant and consider it in conjunction with the rest of God's message in order to apply it to our own lives. Other verses like Jeremiah 17:9 and Proverbs 3:5 confirm how deceitful our hearts can be and warn us not to rely on our own understanding. If our hearts can really mislead us, then it is possible to be fooled into thinking we are motivated by following God's will when in fact it is fueled instead by our selfish desires or human wisdom. I had to face my own deceitful heart in those days of pondering God's purpose in my suffering (and still often do), questioning whether my passion to return to the overseas mission field was specifically God's will or my own self-righteousness. Perhaps it was a 'god of my own making' that I believed had made this all-important plan for my life. In humility, I had to ask myself the question that maybe we all have: *How was it that I, a created being, could hold the Creator God of the universe accountable for 'messing up' my life by bringing me into the crucible of cancer?*

Ironically, I had long ago asked God to give me hardships through which I could grow deeper in my understanding of Him, yet when they came, I did not want to accept them from His hand. Trials like cancer had thrown my faith into a tailspin. Though I still held to the belief that He could use hard things to fashion my heart and soul into something usable for His kingdom, I just couldn't fathom why the Lord would ordain my suffering in such a way that it prevented me from being used in His work as before. Vacillating between the choice of faith in God's will or in my own will, I reasoned that it is true that He wants all people everywhere, even at the 'ends of the earth', to hear His message of Good News. My husband and I had been called to do it; of that, there was no mistake. Yet when cancer came along, my self-perceived purpose in life felt threatened by the possibility of never finishing the evangelism work I felt called to complete. But I had not considered that perhaps my time there was meant to be shorter than I wanted. When I first left for the overseas mission field, I was prepared to live out my days there, but maybe this was not God's plan for me. Perhaps my job was to plant the initial seed of faith, and others to water it and watch it grow in God's grace. I conceded that I would have to ultimately let go of my own plans for a fulfilling future and allow the Lord to reveal His more fitting designs.

While the circuitous nature of God's will for our lives is probably nothing we would ever choose for ourselves (had we known it in advance), we do know that His plans work out for our good, as His beloved children:

> "For we know that God causes all things to work together for good to those who love God, to those who are called according to His purpose." (Romans 8:28, NASB)

In my mental and spiritual struggle to understand God's greater purpose for suffering, I wouldn't rest until I found satisfactory answers. I could not cognitively accept a game-changer like cancer as God's will without being able to reconcile it with what I knew of the character of God. So I pressed on in study, wrestling with the intertwining elements of fact and faith. I had learned from examining how God had worked in the lives of Bible characters that He was ultimately sovereign. Joseph of the Old Testament was one example; a young man whose prime years were wasted in cruel slavery and wrongful imprisonment. Yet later in his life, he was able to testify to his brothers who had misused him that what they had meant for evil, God had purposed for good (paraphrased, from Genesis 50:15-20). To me, that meant that He also ordered and presided over everything that happened both in my life and in the lives of the people to whom I had been called. I had to admit that the Lord did not *need* to use my family to reach people on the other side of the globe. He chose to include us, for a time. If we could not go back to finish what we had started, the Lord would use others instead (and indeed He has).

I decided that to find true hope in this season, I needed to focus more on what was still possible, instead of the things I had lost, which seemed impossible to regain. It was attainable to grow closer to Jesus Christ, my Savior, and to experience His love and goodness more specifically through this trial. After all, it would be preparation for heaven, where I would spend eternity in intimacy with Him! I knew it was also vital in my healing process to receive, with grace, the love and care of my friends and family. As a wife and mother, it had always been second nature for me to serve instead of receive from my family. But I recognized that they all needed to be involved in supporting me through my cancer journey, just as much as I needed their help. For in families we never suffer alone. Our pain affects each loved one uniquely, and it is important for each of them to walk that road along with us, not feel like helpless bystanders. How often we deny our family and friends that integral opportunity by enduring our suffering on our own, cloaked in the reasoning that we don't want to burden others. While they obviously cannot take away our pain or lighten our losses (though they would wish it so), their loving presence can be viewed as extensions of God's nearness to us, bringing us priceless comfort and peace amidst our suffering.

The pastime of reading also brought me comfort during those long days of my cancer recovery. I devoured another missionary biography of a favorite author, Elisabeth Elliot. Have you ever experienced a beloved author become like a close friend you've never met? Elisabeth was such a companion to me, writing with a depth of understanding as she overcame the death of her first husband, Jim Elliot, a missionary martyr in Ecuador. Shocking the world by forgiving his tribal murderers and eventually living among them in order to share the Gospel and translate the Bible into their language, this woman had always embodied for me the courageous faith I fought for. The following quote from her hard-earned wisdom was scribbled down amidst my journaled thoughts:

"I find that faith is more vigorously exercised when I can find no satisfying explanation for the way God does things. I have to hope, without any evidence seen, that things will come right in the end—not merely that we shall receive compensation, but that we and all creation will be redeemed. This means infinitely more than the good will eventually outweigh the evil."[3]

Searching for proof of God's goodness to me in the past buoyed me up toward faith in His present and future goodness. I could ultimately cling to the fact that His life-preserving character would never change, even though my circumstances do. If I put the full weight of my trust in who He was, and is, and forever will be, then I would find Him to be fully faithful. I will admit it is simpler to trust in doctors' prognoses and medical treatments than to trust God with the threatening unknowns of a future beyond my

---

3   Elisabeth Elliot to "Dearest Mother," 30 Nov. 1961, qtd. in *Becoming Elisabeth Elliot*, by Ellen Vaughn, B&H Publishing, 2020.

control. I am honestly still struggling to insert faith into the temptations that come often to resent God for the hard things I've endured. Yet I am taking the opportunity these temptations often give me to pause and ponder hope-filled truths from the Bible and review His good hand in my life over the years. Then I find renewed strength *in Him*, and the wearying road I have trodden seems not quite so long.

Even after treatment, the threat of recurring cancer was to remain my unwelcome companion for years to come. Checkups for recurrence came two to four times a year for the first five years after diagnosis. I was living with "questionable" lymph nodes that had to be routinely scanned, sometimes biopsied, and every time I walked into the cancer center for a follow-up appointment, I was reminded by my doctor that I could not assume my cancer was in remission without five to ten years of no changes on the ultrasound. Mine had been diagnosed as a fairly invasive, though slow-growing thyroid cancer. Along with other debilitating, chronic health issues lingering, I was no longer sure that my stamina could sustain the challenges of life overseas. As of this writing, my family has not been able to move back overseas, though we've continued the Bible curriculum translation work remotely as much as we've been able. Missing our jungle community and the simpler life we had there, we constantly fight the battle to be content with our new situation. Yes, I have stubbornly resisted the reality that we may never return to our work overseas, but I also now believe I can live a purposeful life here in the States, for as long as God wants us here. My five children, "third culture kids" for whom the United States was practically a foreign country when we first returned, have had to overcome some seemingly insurmountable struggles to make this place feel like "home." Yet all have begun to thrive here as young adults. We will be eternally grateful that our family took the extra time together, which we had here for that difficult transition.

My husband recalls a particular jungle vine on the trails from our years in Papua that he and his buddies facetiously called a "wait-a-moment." It is the rattan vine, the same plant that gives us luxurious furniture, but in its natural state, it is quite a force to be reckoned with. A full crown of barbed thorns completely surrounds the vine in 5-inch intervals along the stem. It hangs inconspicuously from the low branches above the trail, waiting to snag the next passerby in its ruthless trap. When the small, thorny claws grab your hat, or worse, your flesh, it takes more than a moment to carefully unhook each double-edged barb. It becomes a hard stop, an unwelcome and unanticipated interruption, similar to a diagnosis of cancer.

One can choose to curse their limiting circumstances, losing momentum and hope, or look for the gift of grace to be found in the waiting. Throughout my cancer journey, my own discouraging circumstances and nagging doubts about God's intentions threatened to squelch my faith and steal my joy for living. But I didn't let it. Like an archeologist who at first finds very little tangible evidence to build their presumptions upon, I dug deep for answers to some of life's hardest questions, scoured the Bible for substantial facts about God's ways, and wrestled my way through misconceptions about my identity and purpose in the world. Though this eternal heart work was often agonizing, I found it to be a worthwhile way to spend the endless days in bed recovering from treatment. It was rewarding to uncover nuggets of truth I could build my faith upon as I mined God's Word for evidence of His goodness, His loving purpose, and His passion for my life to be used for His glory through means far beyond my comprehension. My cancer diagnosis could have left me broken and embittered, as the life plans on which I had constructed false hopes were shattered. But in God's grace, my identity is being renewed as I rest in the truth that I am His beloved child, an individual made in the likeness of Christ, who subjected Himself to being broken and resurrected to new life. For my restless, wandering heart, that gift of hope and eternal perspective has made all the difference.

Next Steps

What about you? If you're reading this book, you may already be familiar with the physical suffering cancer brings into your own life (or that of someone you love). You may have already wrestled with hard questions like those I've mentioned or may still be seeking some satisfying answers. Either way, it may be useful to journal, think, and pray as you reflect on some of the following prompts:

1. In what ways do you need not only physical healing but healing in the deeper issues of the heart? Pray for specifics and write down what those issues are as they come to mind.

2. How has your experience of suffering held you back from living the life you thought God had promised

you? Lay this honestly before God, asking Him to show you how He may want to reframe your suffering and your understanding of His will.

3. Jot down the main messages that occupy your thought life. Are they focused on what you have lost/may lose? What benefits do you see for this time to slow down and focus on the important aspects of life? There are surely many blessings still within your grasp. List these "gifts of grace" and thank God for them.

4. Are there ways that you are judging God's character based on your circumstances? Now turn this around and tell your circumstances who your God is!

Chapter 5

Cancer Sucks, But Your Life Doesn't Have To!

By Julie Stapleton

"I KNOW THAT YOU CAN DO ALL THINGS, AND THAT NO PURPOSE OF YOURS CAN BE THWARTED." JOB 42:2 (ESV)

August 19, 2024 was a day that changed my life forever. I remember that day clearly. I was running errands, checking things off my list of things to do. Our oldest son had just graduated from college. Our youngest son was starting his first day of his junior year at college and had just sent me a required first day of school picture. My husband and I celebrated our 25th wedding anniversary five days prior, and we were planning a much-anticipated anniversary trip. Now, after a routine mammogram, I get the dreaded call, "Mrs. Stapleton, we found something out of the ordinary on your mammogram and we would like for you to come in for an ultrasound." How could this be?!

Fortunately, I was able to get an ultrasound and a subsequent biopsy that same week. I had just started my new job and was in orientation when I received another awful phone call. Unfortunately, the biopsy confirmed there were two malignant tumors in my left breast and one malignant lymph node. Crying or screaming wasn't an option—I had to return to orientation immediately. When I got home, I broke down and hugged my husband, asking why me. At only fifty-five, this was devastating.

After the initial shock wore off, I got busy trying to survive. I called a well-known cancer treatment facility in our area to make an appointment with an oncologist. As a nurse in the area for twenty-six years, I always knew if I were ever diagnosed with cancer, this was the hospital I would choose. Many great hospitals and physicians treat cancer, but this one was close to home, and choosing it helped reduce the stress we were about to endure.

I was able to get an appointment, but it wasn't for three weeks. If you have ever been diagnosed with cancer or know someone who has, you know that waiting is the worst! We made an appointment with a breast surgeon as well because I knew I wanted a mastectomy immediately. After meeting with the oncologist and the surgeon, they made the decision to begin chemotherapy first, with any potential surgeries to come later. The oncologist said HER2+ is a very fast-growing, aggressive cancer, but the good news was that it is now curable. As of 2013, there was a cure. What did this mean? Why couldn't I have a mastectomy first to get these lymph nodes and tumors out of me? We had so many questions! My doctor told us this would be a year-long process or more, with doctor's appointments, infusions, diagnostic studies, and multiple surgeries.

As I began to share my new diagnosis, I quickly realized I wasn't alone. A few friends and co-workers had walked this journey before me, and began to provide mentorship. One of the best pieces of advice I received was for someone to attend my first few appointments with me. I hardly remember my first appointment; it all seems like a big blur. There really is so much to learn. Fortunately, my husband took good notes.

Almost immediately, it became very overwhelming as I learned what the next year of my life would look like. Those who know me know I am a control freak. I have lists of things to do, and I enjoy checking things off my lists. I plan our family calendar a year in advance. Quickly, it became clear this would not be possible for the next year. The phone was ringing off the hook, and email messages were coming through with appointment times faster than I could save them. Despite being a nurse, the terminology and medicines were mostly new to me, as oncology was not my area of expertise.

I was so angry, scared, confused, and shocked. I couldn't believe this was happening. I couldn't understand why God "gave me cancer." I had worked hard, lived right, raised two good kids, and had other health issues that I took on with grace. This was supposed to be our time to travel and do what we wanted as empty nesters. There are 5 stages of grief: denial, anger, bargaining, depression, and acceptance. I remember going through the first four stages multiple times. I didn't stay in the denial and anger phases for long. I quickly began the bargaining phase, telling God I would pray more, go to church more regularly, and read the Bible.

One of the most amazing parts of going to a cancer center is the patients. I never wanted to work in oncology because I assumed it would be too depressing. What I learned was that "cancer patients" are some of the most positive and hopeful people I have ever met. Beginning with the first encounter, from the front door to each and every department, you see eye contact and smiling faces. People greet you in the elevator, say good morning in the lab, make jokes and laugh in the waiting room, and help you if needed. The reason I say, if needed, is because other patients seem to understand that not everyone welcomes advice. If you ask, they are willing and able to help, but they don't offer any unsolicited advice. They know it takes time to process, and everyone processes in their own time and may just need quiet. I believe this is a cancer patient's superpower. The other realization we discovered was hopefulness and gratefulness. I have not encountered one single person who has complained. Each and every patient says mostly the same thing: "It beats the alternative!" Everyone agrees, it is a gift and a blessing to have the opportunity to be treated and to live. I want to thank each and every doctor, surgeon, nurse, staff member, and valet for making this experience easier and for their time and talents.

Soon after I was diagnosed, I began saying "our diagnosis," because if you are lucky enough to have a support system, everyone is involved and feels the pain and the struggles with you. Calling it our diagnosis helped a lot. It didn't feel so lonely for me, and it included my family in our fight. They were suffering as well. Quickly, we realized we were not alone. So many people of all ages have cancer! I made so many friends, shared my story, and listened to theirs. One in particular became a very good friend. We don't share the same cancer, but our personalities are very similar. Two tough women fighting a battle that we ultimately didn't know we would win or lose, but we were determined to fight with grace and grit. We still talk to this day and will be friends for the rest of our lives.

Fighting cancer is a process, and some may call it their journey. I decided it was not my journey, it was my mission. It was my mission to beat cancer. My journey would begin after I beat cancer. I wanted to handle this with grace and poise. I wanted to make my family proud. I was determined not to be depressed, but I have to admit, it crept in occasionally.

My best advice for anyone who gets diagnosed or for a family member who knows someone who is diagnosed is to find out as much information as you can and listen. What does this mean? For me, it meant listening to my physicians. I chose to go with traditional medicine. I am not opposed to a more natural approach or something out of the ordinary, but if there is a cure, I wanted to try that first. If traditional medicine didn't work, then we were planning to be more aggressive and ask about trials and other non-traditional approaches.

Something else that helped was listening to other cancer patients' stories and sharing mine. I didn't get on a lot of social media groups. I wanted to keep my circle smaller. But I learned a lot from the waiting rooms. Sharing your story helps you learn and helps others as well. It created a commonality and normalized our diagnosis. Maybe someday I will join some groups in our community, church, or on social media, but it was already so overwhelming. A mentor is so important when you are facing something unknown. Again, my circle was small by choice, but it was solid.

My next piece of advice is to let people help you. They feel helpless and confused as well, and they want to help. I am blessed to have so many friends and family who supported both my husband and me through our mission to fight cancer. I was also fortunate enough to have regular texts from these people to check in and let me know they would do anything we needed.

Lastly, I advise everyone to pray, read scripture, and attend church regularly. This helped me a lot! I began praying and reading scripture. Job was recommended to me by my son, and it seemed the most fitting, so I started there. God has a plan for each of us, but we are often in the dark about what our future holds. I needed answers, and my prayers began to change. No longer was I simply expressing thankfulness and listing my requests. I began to ask God the hard questions for which I had no answers. Had I already made my mark on life? What do people think about me? Is my legacy my children? Did I make a difference in life at work? Or is cancer my new beginning and legacy? I began to slow down and be less busy. I began to truly listen for God's response. This new focus on God and His plan for my life led to an inner peace I had never experienced before. Through prayer, family, church and church friends, work friends, and new friends, I began accepting my diagnosis and the unknown.

Cancer was a gift, and it has changed my life forever for the better. I have made new forever friends, reacquainted with old friends, and grown so much closer to my husband and family. When most people die, they aren't ready. They don't know who will attend their funeral or what will be said after they are gone. I was lucky. I learned who I could count on, who I had impacted, and how. I found out what people think of me and the legacy I had already left. My new diagnosis changed my perspective and made me slow down, and I enjoyed every single day. I wake up with a smile each and every morning and thank God for this life. The little things that used to upset me don't anymore. I am grateful!

Next Steps

God's plans cannot be stopped. What He intends will happen. Job 42:2 (ESV) says: "I know that you can do all things, and that no purpose of yours can be thwarted." If something doesn't go the way we expected, it's because His greater purpose is at work. Peace comes from trusting that nothing escapes His control. In life, we face adversity and challenges, and we must continue to keep our faith in God. We should seek to serve God, live intentionally, and wake up each and every morning thanking God for this beautiful life. I believe God chose me and gave me this opportunity to share my joy and happiness, even in the worst of times. Cancer sucks, but your life doesn't have to.

Chapter 6

Scary Doctor

By Susan Laurie Hutchinson

"FEAR OF MAN WILL PROVE TO BE A SNARE, BUT THOSE WHO TRUST IN THE LORD WILL BE KEPT SAFE." PROVERBS 29:25 (NIV)

Way back in 1989, I read a book.

After I read the last page, I studied the woman pictured on the cover with sadness and thought, *Wow! THAT'S something you don't want to get. That's a killer!* The book was called *It's Always Something*, an autobiography by Gilda Radnor, one of Saturday Night Live's original funny ladies. Gilda died at the age of forty-three from ovarian cancer.

And here I was, many years later, in Gilda's shoes.

Life was good. Our three kids were married, lived locally, and were filling our lives with the happy sound of grandkids running through the house. So, in 2007, my husband Mike and I purchased a beach property for family vacations. We spent the whole first year renovating the house together. Our favorite evenings were spent walking on the beach to the end of the island and back, about a mile. By the summer of 2009, this became a chore for me, as I would walk half the distance and look up the beach towards The Point, only to think how nice it would be to just lie down in the sand. That's when I took note—not only was I tired and losing weight, but I had constant backaches. I chalked my lack of appetite to severe acid reflux because nothing seemed to agree with me. In August, after gallstones appeared on an ultrasound, I had my gallbladder removed. I will always be thankful for that surgery because it was the gallbladder surgeon who saw something amiss and pointed me in the right direction.

During the surgery, a mass was discovered around my right ovary. When I awoke, he gave me a script for a pelvic ultrasound and requested the results be sent to my gynecologist. Even so, I was unprepared when my GYN called and insisted I see her immediately. I already had a routine appointment scheduled with her for the following week. When I came into the office, my doctor had me lined up that same afternoon with an oncology gynecologist and a surgical date.

Things went from bad to worse all in one short afternoon. From the beach to the operating room in less than two weeks. My head was spinning, and I didn't have time to process the quick turn of events!

Oh yeah, I've been there ... and maybe you have too.

Watching the oncology doctor move his lips and hearing his words was almost a surreal experience. I sat on the exam table, clenching and unclenching my hands, flipping them around, palms together, then not, twisting my fingers, trying to grasp the significance of what the doctor was saying. I cocked my head to the side and furrowed my brow as I studied his face, that only an hour before was new to me. He was now my new best friend. Watching his lips move, I knew he was talking about me, but I had trouble absorbing and relating to the words. I kept glancing at my husband as if to ask, "Can you believe what the doctor is saying about me?" but Mike was intent on the words he was hearing.

The CA125 blood test is the cancer marker for ovarian and pancreatic cancer. The normal number is under 20; my number was in the high 400s. The two possibilities were dismal, to say the least. I was scheduled for surgery the following week and went home to wait for more test results.

For the next three days, pancreatic cancer was the elephant in the room that Mike and I didn't discuss. We circled around the unspoken fear, passing each other with a soft touch or stopping for a hug. His cousin had passed away earlier in the year from pancreatic cancer, so it was heavy on our minds. The irony of the relief I felt wasn't lost on me when the doctor called and said it wasn't pancreatic. The odds of surviving ovarian cancer weren't a lot better, but at least now I knew my enemy.

Well, not really. All I knew about ovarian cancer was what I read twenty-five years ago in Gilda Radner's book. And there was no good news to be found there. No happy ending. I made the mistake of googling survival statistics in the first days, and what I read seared my brain like cattle branding. Only 20% make it five years. Ovarian cancer usually returns in eighteen months. I slammed my computer closed with a bang and decided on two things then and there.

The first was that I was never researching ovarian cancer again. I was done with Dr. Google. My friends could do it and spoon-feed me any good news. Instead, I decided to heed the words of Mark Twain, who said, "Be careful about reading health books. You may die of a misprint."[4] I thought that was sound advice, and it applied to the internet! Once you read it, you own it, and I wasn't going down that road.

I decided to focus on the 20% who survive for five years. *Why can't that be me? Why do I have to assume I will be part of the 80% that don't?*

The question is ... How do you prepare for that kind of news? No one is prepared when they're blindsided. I was face-to-face with a Goliath of a killer, and I am no David. At least I wasn't then. This was a surprise attack that came from nowhere. I felt unprepared and unarmed. I thought about my life being over, my husband a widower in his 50s, my children distraught, and my grandchildren who would never remember me. We had also adopted a family from Sri Lanka into ours, and they were due to arrive in a few weeks. I thought, *Lord, did you bring them here to take me out now?* My grief was deep and wide, and I couldn't seem to get a grip.

But I was more prepared than I thought.

I have an army of prayer warriors and the armor of God. I have 40 years of walking with Jesus and a lifetime of positive thinking. I have sisters to care for me, children to do for me, and grandchildren to love on me. I have friends who cook for me and a husband who listens to me. Years of Bible teaching and life experiences help with perspective. Facing the enemy is easier on some days than others; there's no denying it. Moving past the devastation of hard facts takes time. But as

---

4 Commonly attributed to Mark Twain; original source unverified.

it turned out, there were more than a few smooth stones in my pouch to slay the giant. The giant I was facing was fear.

Mentally, I reached into that pouch to test the weight of those stones. I counted them one by one and felt the firm, solid weight of my arsenal. My confidence grew until I could say, like David did when he stood before the Philistine giant, "Oh no ... You come up against me with resistant cancer cells, lousy survival statistics, and energy-draining chemo, but I come against you in the name of the Lord Almighty, the God of the armies of Israel!"

Now, I don't want you to think this was easy-peasy.

I was scared of everything: scared of the process, scared of the chemo, scared of the side effects, scared of the statistics, scared of the surgery and the hospital, scared for my family, and scared of the doctor because everything that came out of his mouth was scary and new. I felt the weight of my future, my very life, lay in his hands. I vaguely wondered how he carried the weight of all his patients on his shoulders because I knew they were expecting him to have the answers, just like I was.

The only thing I wasn't scared of was dying. I have full confidence in my eternal future with the Lord. That's all good and to be looked forward to, like when I'm about 95, as planned. What is the saying, "Man plans and God laughs?" The thought of leaving behind my whole and happy life filled me with overwhelming grief. I couldn't imagine God laughing at that.

I went into surgery, not certain I would wake up. The tumor was the size of a brick and pressed on an artery that, when removed, could cause a fatal blood clot. To prevent that from happening, I went a day early to have a surgical procedure to insert a screen in my vein to catch clots. The next day, I underwent surgery for a complete hysterectomy and the removal of three enlarged lymph nodes, one the size of a baseball, pressing against my diaphragm.

When I awoke from surgery, my favorite person's eyes locked into mine. The doctor had told Mike I wouldn't wake up for a while, so he was surprised when I smiled and asked … "Was it cancer?" I still held out hope. He held my hand and nodded with a quiet yes.

> "Oh," I replied. And like King Hezekiah, who became ill to the point of death, I turned my face to the wall and prayed. (2 Kings 20:1-4, NIV)

Every morning around 6:30 a.m., my doctor would make rounds with a group of residents, answer my questions, and inform me of any developments with test results or consults he had with his team. I anticipated his visits with a mixture of hope and dread, and in my mind, I tagged him The Scary Doctor because it seemed as if everything that came out of his mouth was scary! I called Mike and said, "You have to be here at 6:30 am tomorrow because The Scary Doctor is making his rounds! And sure enough, Mike would be there to listen and ask questions. Residents would make rounds as well during the day, answering questions.

That is when we learned that because the cancer had traveled out of the peritoneal cavity, I was stage 4. Dr. Edelson said he did not remove my omentum (a fatty tissue that drapes over the intestines), even though it contained cancer cells, because he thought the chemo would take care of it.

And then he also gave us the news that my type of cancer was of a clear cell nature, often resistant to chemotherapy. Dr Edelson was kind, gentle in his delivery, and caring enough not to rush us through questions, but you can understand why I referred to him as scary. Hence his tag name, "Scary Doctor!"

I was in the hospital for about a week with lots of time to think. I'm not much of a TV watcher, but I love to read. I had my Bible with me, and I came across Proverbs 29:25. It caught my attention, and I went back and read it again. "Fear of man will prove to be a snare, but those who trust in the Lord will be kept safe." (Proverbs 29:25, NIV)

I found a pen and wrote the Proverb on a napkin from dinner. I read it again. And again. And again. I put the napkin on my table and reread it at least twenty times until it dawned on me that my fear of "man" was getting in my way. I knew Dr Edelson was undoubtedly my advocate; his reputation as a skilled, patient, and thorough surgeon was researched and reported to me by my friend, a nurse who worked in the same hospital and asked nurses who worked with him in the operating room. He never made me feel like a number or simply a name on the chart. He thoughtfully considered each question. He smiled and had a nice manner about him.

What was my problem?

I wanted him to have all the answers, but the truth is, despite his vast knowledge on the subject, his medical experience and expertise, his research and board sitting, and his in-depth study of the field, he is only a man, not God. I can rely on all of the above and depend on his expert opinion and guidance, but ultimately, my trust needs to be in the Lord, not a man. Even one as gifted as Dr Edelson. I would question and listen to the answers I was given, but I also needed to listen to and trust in God.

With that realization, all the weight of responsibility I had placed on the shoulders of "Scary Doctor" fell off. We were both free, but only I knew of the shift.

For the most part, the fear left me. I would still feel a flutter of unease within me when he made rounds, but calm was the new reigning feeling. Rationality ruled. The funny thing was, I knew my fear wasn't rational but emotional. But fear is fear and needs to be addressed if you want to move on and not live there. If I wasn't going to be around long, I wanted to enjoy my life.

Going home, I had wonderful support from family and friends. Meals were cooked for us, cards and letters arrived, and friends came and rocked on my front porch. The recovery hours at home passed by pleasantly.

During the day, that is.

At night, I would lie awake for hours, gazing through our bedroom window at the night sky above the neighbor's barn. I could NOT pray. I was stuck on "Help me, Lord." I cried the night through, wondering if I should give away my jewelry, clean out my closets, or write letters to my grandkids. I also would sometimes call my friend at 2 am while she was working the night shift in Labor and Delivery and spill out the grief I didn't want to burden Mike with. He had enough on his plate.

My kids kicked into gear. One made my doctor appointments for second and third opinions; one set up a website for me to be able to communicate what was going on with our huge family and many friends. My daughter called me every morning at 8:30 am on her way to work. The phone would ring, and I'd hear her cheerful voice ask, "Ok, Mom, are you ready for your morning prayer?" And she would pray all those things my mind couldn't formulate. I would wake up and look at that phone, willing it to ring each morning!

During the six weeks of recovery, my daughter had scheduled second and third opinions from two other renowned hospitals, Johns Hopkins and the University of Pennsylvania. All three hospitals offered the same standard treatment, but at the University of Pennsylvania, the head of the department, Dr. Rubin, suggested a clinical trial for me. Well, I am all for clinical trials because back in the 1980s, my father had a brain tumor and was given three months to live. He qualified for a clinical trial at Hahnemann Hospital and went on to live nine more years. My nephew, at the age of five, had Ewing Sarcoma, qualified for a trial, and is now thirty-seven. So I heard about clinical trials and said, "Sign me up!"

Clinical trials have stringent guidelines. Everyone in the trial has to fall within certain criteria for each trial, and I was told I had to wait eight weeks to get into this particular trial, which was recommended. By week seven, I had not heard. So I picked up the phone and called the University of Pennsylvania, and spoke to the nurse. She said, "I'm sorry. It looks like you are not going to get into this trial after all. But you can still come here for chemotherapy." I was devastated! I gave a half-hearted okay, but when I hung up the phone, I put my head on the desk in despair and asked, "Lord. Now, what do I do?" I just stayed there.

Within two minutes, the phone rang. I lifted my head and answered the phone. It was Dr. Edelson from Abington Hospital where I had my surgery. The first words out of his mouth were "Susan, this is Dr. Edelson. I've been thinking about you."

He explained that a clinical trial came across his desk that I would qualify for, and he thought it was a good fit for me. My heart leapt with joy!! Yes, sign me up! I got off the phone and called the University of Pennsylvania hospital and got the nurse. I explained to her about the clinical trial at Abington. She asked me what the trial was. I told her, and she asked me to wait while she put me on hold. I waited.

When the nurse came back to the phone, she reported they had the same trial at the University of Pennsylvania, and did I want to come there? Shocked, I replied, "No, thank you. I'm going where the doctor was thinking about me." I hung up, leaped from the chair, and laughed out loud in amazement as I thought about what had just transpired. Going from my head on the desk in a tearful, forlorn prayer to a phone call from Dr. Edelson filled me with hope and possibility. God heard the cry of my heart! Also, after my initial meeting with Dr. Rubin at the University of Pennsylvania, I didn't speak with him again. I dealt with the nurse. Yet Dr. Edelson called me himself. *That* was the doctor I wanted in my camp.

Ha! He's not so scary after all!

Mike rarely left my side during that time. One day, as I walked through the family room, he was reading his Bible. He slammed it shut, stood up, and pointed at me, asking, "Susan, is our faith in God based on who He is or on what He can do for us?"

Is this a trick question? I wondered as I gazed at my husband in puzzlement.

I knew he was having his own struggle with my cancer diagnosis and uncertain future. He told me once, quite recently, that he used to think he wanted to be the first to go, to die before me, but has since changed his mind because he wants to spare me that kind of pain. Here we are, each wanting to help the other, but are uncertain how to proceed. This is new, uncharted territory.

I looked at his face now. Gone was the quick smile, the reason for the crinkly lines around his blue eyes. What I saw instead was the expectation of an answer. So I gave him one.

"In who He is."

"That's right", he said with conviction, brushing past me with a kiss on the cheek. "It's in who He is."

Left alone in the room, I sank onto the sofa, grabbed a pillow, and bunched it against my stomach. I leaned over and buried my face in it, but I could still hear the ticking of the seven-day clock on the kitchen wall. Ticking away the minutes of my life.

On the surface, the question was simple, but my deep faith in God was suddenly called into question. My anchor had torn loose with the proclamation of stage 4 ovarian cancer, and I was set adrift, swirling around in a vortex of information, decision-making, and impending loss. Night after night, I lay in bed, trying to pray, but I was stuck. Stalled in inertia. I longed for health and healing, but couldn't formulate a prayer.

So there I sat, pondering the question. What is my faith based on?

When tragedy strikes, many people lose their faith. How can a benevolent God let bad things happen to them and those they love? Obviously, I wanted health and healing, and many people were praying for me, but what if I didn't get the results I wanted? I had to decide. Either I trusted God, or I didn't. If my faith is truly based on who He is and not on what He can do for me, then I have to be okay with the outcome no matter what.

This was big. No matter what.

Slowly, I sat up, and a feeling of quiet reflection and contentment settled over me like a warm blanket. I smiled to myself as I thought about my husband, who, from the heart of his great faith and love for me, caused me to examine mine, and once again, I drifted into a time of peace.

As I would lie wide awake in bed at night, I began to think about my father. The memory that came to me was of a time I went to visit him in the hospital near the end of his life. My mom went to get some coffee, and I had him all to myself. He was lying in his hospital bed, hooked up to all kinds of machines, and had his eyes closed. I leaned over the bed to talk to him. I told him what a great Dad he had always been, what a powerful influence he had on my life, and how much I loved him. He never stirred or opened his eyes. Then I said, "Hey, Dad, remember how you always said how great life is?" and with that, he opened his eyes, smiled at me, and said, "It is," and closed his eyes. I thought to myself, "Wow, he can still say that while he is hooked up to all these things and in so much pain."

I remembered him standing in the bathroom every morning after showering, with a towel wrapped around him, shaving before putting on his suit for work. He would sing as he shaved, and the singing would always draw me in. I would be racing up and down the stairs, getting ready for school, but would often pause to lean against the bathroom door and listen to him bellow out old hymns in his baritone, amused at his daily routine. The words of some of the hymns he sang came back to me. Beloved songs of my childhood and teen years.

'What a friend we have in Jesus. All our sins and griefs to bear. What a privilege to carry everything to God in prayer.'[5] And what would follow was, *Jesus, are you my friend? I really need you to be my friend.*

"Have we trials and temptations? Is there trouble everywhere? We should never be discouraged; take it to the Lord in prayer."[6] And in my head, with a bit of an attitude, I'd respond *Yeah, this is a bit of a trial! I'm in trouble! Do you hear me? Will you help me?*

"Standing on the promises of Christ my King. Through eternal ages, let His praises ring. Glory in the highest I will shout and sing. Standing on the promises of God!"[7] And I would mull over the promises written in the Bible ... *What are your promises, God? Well, your word says you will never leave me nor forsake me. That when I walk through the fire, you will be with me.* (Isaiah 43:2, NIV) *That if I have the faith of a mustard seed, I can move mountains* (Matt 17:20, NIV).

---

5   Joseph Scriven, "What a Friend We Have in Jesus," 1855.
6   Scriven, "What a Friend We Have in Jesus."
7   Russell Carter, "Standing on the Promises," 1886.

Well, I think I have that much faith ... I may even have a little more than that.

"Great is thy faithfulness. Great is thy faithfulness. Morning by morning, new mercies, I see. All I have needed thy hands have provided. Great is thy faithfulness, Lord unto me."[8] *Well, God, this is a new morning, and I need your new mercies. I need a new mercy to be able to get out of bed, walk down the hall, and put one foot in front of the other. I need your new mercies to be able to put a smile on my face, so I am not crying all the time. I need your faithfulness, Lord.*

And you know what began to happen? The words of those old songs and many more became my prayers as I remembered one after the other. I would lie in bed and sing them, and those beautiful words opened up the floodgates of my prayer life once again.

Mike said, "I hear you singing."

"I'm praying", I replied.

And I climbed out of the pit little by little, one song, one prayer at a time!

It's been a lot of years since then—sixteen, to be exact. I am long past the every-three-month routine of CA125 blood tests and CAT scans. Even after my schedule went to every six months, I cried through every CAT scan. The technician would always ask if I was okay, and I would always say, "Yes, I just can't believe I'm here." That same feeling followed me down the hall every time I walked under the Hanjani Cancer Center sign to go to chemotherapy. But as I sat in the chair and my port was being accessed, I would say to the nurse,

---

8   Thomas Chisholm, "Great Is Thy Faithfulness," 1923.

"I know that's poison you're giving me, but I believe it's the healing blood of Jesus running through my veins."

Now, I just go once a year for a blood test and an office visit. Initially, Dr. Edelson would call me with results, and that same old familiar anxiety would grip me when I saw his name on the screen. Then we moved to online portals, and now I get an email saying my test results are in. Same deal. It's "Drum roll, please," as I open the portal. Maybe that feeling of uncertainty will never go away. But I will never tire of the elation I feel when I see the low number. My reaction is always a shout of joy, a clap of the hands, a fist thrust in the air.

I don't know why I'm one of the fortunate ones. I have no answer. I have a good doctor who looks out for me. I have an attitude of gratitude for every day, week, month, and year I'm given. I've fought enough battles in my life for things that mattered to know that faith in the fight is important. It's my history with the Lord and how He shows up that reminds me time and again that I am not alone. "The Lord will fight for you if you only be still." (Exodus 14:14, NIV)

And the clincher is Psalm 46:10 (NIV), "Be still, and know that I am God," because it's in the stillness we hear His voice.

Things I Learned That Might Help You

1. Steer clear of googling your symptoms, your diagnosis, or other people's experiences with what you are going through. Misinformation abounds, and all it does is feed your worry and insecurity. It takes intention to focus your thoughts on the positive, but

it is possible, even necessary, if we want a renewed and steadfast spirit. (Psalm 51:10, NIV)

2. Establish your posse of friends and family you can count on. One thing cancer does is showcase those you can depend on. Everyone means well, but not everyone is capable of the support you need. Some friends will rally behind you while others don't know how to respond. Reactions vary, and people say the dumbest and most thoughtless things. Don't hold it against them, they just don't get it. I had a woman look at me with shock and say, "Wow! That's a death sentence!" when I told her I had stage 4 ovarian cancer. She may as well have smacked me across the face. I had to shake it off, leave it at the table. It wasn't easy, and you can see I haven't forgotten, but I forgave her.

3. Worship. That doesn't just mean on Sunday morning. I filled my iPod with songs of hope and victory that played in my ears all night long as I struggled to pray, then sleep. I played music during the day as I went about my business in the house or spent hours in my sewing room. The result was often an irresistible urge to get to my feet, lift my hands in praise as I'd dance around. As my hands went up, so did my spirits, lifted in thanksgiving for all I've been given in life. More than once, I'd turn to see Mike leaning against the doorjamb, watching me with a smile. Whether I survived long term or not, I could give thanks and praise to a God whom I trusted. Nothing lifts your spirits like true gratitude.

Practical Next Steps You Can Take

1. Create a Playlist of Christian music and inspirational feel-good songs. The songs should include a wide range of topics to cover different kinds of emotional support. For instance, there are songs about how God sees us and hears us. There are fight songs, victory songs, songs of lament, songs about the love of God for his children, and songs of how we love Him back. Go online, listen, and download. As you play them over and over, they become the cry of your heart when you run out of words. Kind of like a cheat sheet.

2. Find a daily devotional you like. Start your day reading it, first thing in the morning. Cry your way through if you must. I did. It helped. My go-to was Jesus Calling by Sarah Young. I was always amazed at how it spoke to what I was feeling.

3. Journal your progress and feelings. I journaled on the website my daughter set up for me to keep everyone apprised of what was going on, and I'm so glad I did. You think you are going to remember everything, but you won't. And maybe you think you don't want to remember, but here's the blessing in remembering. You can look back with ... here I go again ... GRATITUDE for what the Lord has brought you through. I never want to tire of being thankful.

Take one day at a time. Whether it's been a week, a month, or a year since your diagnosis, you are a survivor, so live each day with the expectation of God's best for you.

Chapter 7

A Divine Orchestration: My Journey Through Fear, Faith, and Healing

By Julie O'Dell

"FOR WE WALK BY FAITH, NOT BY SIGHT."
2 CORINTHIANS 5:7 (ESV)

December 2013 – The Pain That Changed Everything

It started as a small, nagging discomfort, something easy to dismiss in the chaos of daily life. A dull ache in my stomach would creep in without warning, sometimes barely noticeable, other times sharp enough to take my breath away.

At first, I ignored it.

Moms don't have time to be sick. I had two young children—a toddler who never napped, and a seven-year-old who needed me to be present. My husband, dedicated to his work as a police officer in a specialized unit, was away for long hours, sometimes days at a time. I was used to juggling everything on my own, telling myself that any pain I felt was just stress.

But deep down, something felt off.

The episodes became more frequent. The pain no longer came and went quietly; it struck without warning, doubling me over, stealing my breath, forcing me to my knees as tears spilled down my face. I tried to push through, clenching my jaw as I cooked dinner, tucked my kids into bed, and kept the household running.

Then came the night at the hockey game.

It was supposed to be a special evening. My husband was home, a rare occurrence, and my entire family was together to watch the game. It was Teddy Bear Toss night, a magical moment where kids could throw stuffed animals onto the ice for charity. My children were thrilled, their excitement infectious.

Then, just as we arrived, the pain struck. I tried so hard to hide it, not wanting to ruin the special night.

It started as a sharp twist in my gut, then intensified until I felt like I was being stabbed from the inside out. I tried to stand, to pretend it was nothing, but within minutes, I was hunched over, arms wrapped around my torso, my knees pressed to my chest as I gasped for air.

"Are you okay?" my husband asked, his voice tight with concern.

I shook my head, biting my lip against the agony. "I" My words caught in my throat. "I need to go to the ER."

Saying those words out loud felt like admitting defeat. Leaving the game crushed me. I didn't want to miss my children's joy and laughter. But I knew something was wrong.

Not to mention I desperately tried to avoid the inconvenience to my husband, who rarely had the chance to see events like this with our kids.

At the ER, the doctor barely looked at me before waving it off as food poisoning, maybe gastritis. "Nothing serious," she said. "It'll pass."

I couldn't understand how this could be and thought she was wrong. That night, I emailed my primary care doctor, demanding an appointment. The earliest they could see me was three and a half months later!

March 31, 2014 – The Appointment That Changed Everything

By the time my appointment rolled around, the pain had mysteriously faded. For weeks, I had been bracing for the next attack, but it never came. A small part of me wondered if the ER doctor had been right. Maybe it was just stress or food poisoning. Still, I kept my appointment.

As I sat in the exam room, I chatted with my doctor about everything except why I was there. We talked about skincare, fashion, and my favorite restaurants. I had almost forgotten about my own health concerns until she suddenly said, "Let's check your stomach real quick."

The second her fingers pressed into my abdomen, she froze.

"What is this?" she murmured.

I sat up, heart pounding. "What is what?" I couldn't believe I forgot to mention my stomach pains, and wondered if this lump could be the culprit of it all.

"There's a small lump here," she said, pressing slightly harder just below my left ribs.

A lump. The word echoed in my mind like a siren.

She straightened, her face unreadable. "It's probably nothing, but I want to schedule an ultrasound just to be sure."

My mouth was dry. "Okay." I immediately did my ultrasound and went home.

A few weeks later, they called and said they needed to schedule an appointment for a needle core biopsy of the area to better identify the lump, as the ultrasound was inconclusive.

May 20, 2014 – The Needle Core Biopsy

The lump hadn't gone away. If anything, it seemed more pronounced. The ultrasound was inconclusive, so my doctor scheduled a biopsy.

The morning of the biopsy, my husband drove me to the hospital. As we walked in, the nurse informed him that he wasn't allowed in the procedure room. "It's routine," she assured him. "It won't take long." I lay on the exam table, the bright surgical light glaring down at me. The doctor walked in, glanced at my chart, and let out a small chuckle.

"Mrs. O'Dell, why is everyone making such a fuss over this?" he asked, shaking his head. My stomach twisted. "Excuse me?" He gestured at the ultrasound image on the screen beside me, his expression calm, almost dismissive. "This is nothing, just your abdominal muscles. You work out, right?" His voice was even, as if he had said this a thousand times before. "That's all this is. It's just your abdominis. It's nothing."

I stared at him, my breath catching in my throat. I wanted to believe him. God, I needed to believe him. But I couldn't.

"I've been having severe stomach pain for months," I said, my voice tight. My fingers dug into the cold edges of the examination table. "If you can look me in the eye and tell me with absolute certainty that this is nothing, I'll leave right now."

He said, "I promise it's nothing."

The fluorescent lights above hummed, casting a sterile glow over the small room. The ultrasound gel clung to my skin, sticky and cool, and the faint beeping of a heart monitor in the next room made me feel like time was stretching thin. I hated being here. I hated the smell of antiseptic, the sharp tang of fear in my throat. I hated needles.

And I hated feeling like a hypochondriac, doubting myself, second-guessing my instincts. But I also needed to be able to look my kids in the eye and tell them I had done everything ... that I had fought for every possible chance to be there for them. Because if I walked away from this, and it turned out to be cancer, and I had waited too long to fight it ... what kind of mother would I be?

I already knew the answer. In that moment, something in me settled. "I want the biopsy."

He exhaled through his nose, rubbing his forehead, then nodded. "Alright." His voice was softer now. "Let's do the biopsy." He glanced at me, and for the first time, I saw something shift in his expression. A flicker of understanding. "I'm really good at what I do, so let's do this if you want it."

I swallowed hard, my pulse thudding in my ears. As the needle slid into my skin, sharp and invasive, I clenched my fists so tightly my nails bit into my palms. A hot sting ran through my abdomen, but I didn't flinch. Instead, I prayed.

Not for an easy answer. Not for the pain to disappear. I prayed for time.

The bible verse Jeremiah 29:11 (NIV) came to mind: "For I know the plans I have for you, declares the Lord, plans to prosper you and not harm you, plans to give you hope and a future."

May 29, 2014 – The Diagnosis

The doctor's hands were shaking when he walked into the room. My husband stood beside me, still in his police uniform. We were expecting quick results, some benign explanation. The doctor pulled his chair close.

"I'm so sorry, honey," he said softly. "It's cancer. A very, very rare type of tumor. We need to schedule surgery immediately."

The world tilted. I couldn't breathe.

He kept talking, but the words blurred together. I caught fragments, a rare tumor ... aggressive ... immediate surgery.

Somewhere in the fog, I heard him say, "I have cancer too. Mine is terminal. Yours is not."

"The tumor has grown and attached to your ribs, so during surgery, we will need to remove some of them as well. This will result in a significant scar, and due to the size and location of the tumor in your abdomen, you may notice some changes in how you move or feel afterward. However, we will have a full surgical team in the room to ensure we achieve good margins. After the procedure, we will discuss your chemotherapy and radiation plan."

The doctor told us to go straight out the door to the right and schedule my surgery with his nurse. He insisted we couldn't leave until the appointment was made. I looked at my husband and said, "I just need a day to process this. I can't schedule it right now."

But my husband shook his head and said, "No, Julie, you need to follow the doctor's orders. We need to do this now." So we did. We walked over to the nurse and scheduled the surgery for about a week later.

We walked out of the hospital in silence. I gripped the steering wheel of my car, hands trembling. Would I live to see my children grow up? Would I make it to their next birthdays? Their graduations? Their weddings? The thoughts were unbearable. I sobbed the entire drive home.

The Stranger Who Changed Everything

A few weeks before my diagnosis, I met a woman named Jane at the park, a complete and total stranger. Our kids played together, and in the midst of our small talk, she asked if we attended church. When I told her we hadn't stepped inside one in two years, she warmly invited us to hers.

At the time, my husband had been hesitant about attending in person. As a police officer, he was always cautious, and with our youngest child still unable to talk, he felt uneasy bringing them into unfamiliar environments.

Until he can tell us if something is wrong, we don't go to church in person, he'd always said.

But something about Jane's invitation lingered in my heart. It felt like a gentle tug, something I couldn't ignore. So, I pleaded with my husband to let us attend church for Mother's Day, as that was the next Sunday, and it would be a wonderful Mother's Day gift. He agreed.

That Sunday, we went. Jane was deeply involved in the church, seemingly knowing everyone. It felt like God had orchestrated our meeting with a purpose. The service filled me with warmth, a sense of belonging after so long away. I didn't know it then, but that simple invitation would become a lifeline.

The Turning Point

Not long after, I received the news that changed everything. When I was diagnosed, Jane was the first person I told outside of my family. I didn't want to burden anyone else, but Jane? She felt like hope. She felt like someone I could trust to get that prayer circle going, without any questions or extra stress.

I called her, my voice shaking. "Jane, I just got terrible news. I'm scared. I need prayer." I knew we had only just met, and to her, I probably seemed like a perfectly healthy mom. But the truth was, I had just received devastating news." Without hesitation, she told me to meet her at church that Sunday, and she would arrange a prayer circle for us.

The days passed in a blur of fear and uncertainty. When Sunday finally came, I arrived at church searching for her, but she was nowhere to be found. A knot tightened in my stomach. Had she forgotten? I barely knew her. Maybe I had put too much trust in a stranger. I felt embarrassed, even foolish, for confiding in her before I'd told my own family.

Just as doubt crept in, my phone rang.

"Julie, where are you? I'm down the hall, in a room by the restrooms, waiting for you."

Relief flooded my heart. We rushed down the hall, and when I opened the door, I was met with something I never expected. Fifty people. Jane had gathered fifty people to pray over me, my husband Tom, my daughter Joy, and my son Christian. She shared my story with them, and together, they pressed their hands to our shoulders, lifting their voices in a beautiful, powerful prayer. I was in tears. At that moment, I felt Jesus. I felt at peace.

"And the peace of God, which surpasses all understanding, will guard your hearts and your minds through Christ Jesus." (Philippians 4:7, NKJV)

The Miracle

Hours later, I received an unexpected call from a woman in that prayer circle. She was an oncology nurse at the same Kaiser I was originally diagnosed at. She told me she knew a doctor who could give me a second opinion that same day if I could get to Kaiser Hospital immediately. It was a chance I hadn't even thought possible. My surgery date had already been set, just days away. The first doctor told me the procedure was urgent, and I had booked it before even leaving his office. Time was everything.

But do you remember my prayer? I had asked God for more time. And in His own mysterious way, He answered.

That second doctor changed everything. He told me something shocking: surgery could actually make my condition worse. The type of tumor I had was known to multiply when disturbed, potentially shutting down my organs and leading to death.

Instead of rushing into surgery, he recommended medication and a wait-and-watch approach.

Had I gone through with the original plan, I might not be here to tell this story.

But God intervened. Through Jane. Through a prayer circle of strangers. Through a phone call that led me to the doctor who would ultimately save my life.

God worked at His speed and in His way. And I am forever grateful.

I left that doctor's office with a renewed sense of hope and joy, but also confusion. How could two doctors from the same hospital have such completely opposite views on my care?

Right away, I emailed the first doctor, the head of surgery, whose office was just a few doors down from the second opinion doctor. I told him I had decided not to go through with the life-changing surgery that was only days away. I thanked him for his time and expertise, but explained that I had chosen a different path for my aggressive, cancerous tumor.

I never got a reply. No email, no phone call. Years later, I learned that he had passed away from his own terminal cancer.

At the time, his silence hurt. I had trusted this man with my life. A young mom with little kids and an incredible husband who supported us with every bone in his body. And yet, in the end, I felt like just another number.

Those who know me know my faith runs deep. I have a testimony to prove it. They also know I'm not quick to take pills or medication unless absolutely necessary. I believe medicine can sometimes create more problems, like a snowball effect where one pill leads to another, and suddenly, you're treating side effects instead of the original issue.

So when I left my second opinion doctor's office, he told me to pick up my prescription, start taking it daily, and in three months, we'd do a scan to see whether the tumor had shrunk or grown. The medication had been shown to shrink tumors like mine, statistically speaking.

I picked up the prescription, but in my heart, I already knew what I was going to do. I was going to set it aside and pray, every single day, that God would heal me. That He would shrink my tumor, and I would sing His praises from the highest places. I promised him that if he healed me without the medication, I would be his vessel, sharing his love and the path he had set for my life.

But I also made a deal with him: If, at the three-month scan, nothing had changed, I would keep trusting. But if at any point the tumor grew, I would take that as my sign to start the medication, following the path he had placed before me. It probably seemed crazy, maybe even stupid to some. But my faith was strong, and I wanted all the glory to go to Jesus.

This was one of the most challenging seasons of my life, I clung to these promises.

I chose to believe that healing could come not through fear, not through chemicals that might harm me more, but through pure, unwavering faith.

These verses reminded me daily that with God, no diagnosis was final and no situation was impossible.

They became the foundation of my hope:

"And whatever you ask in prayer, you will receive, if you have faith." (Matthew 21:22, ESV)

"For nothing will be impossible with God." (Luke 1:37, ESV)

In a world that offered me fear, side effects, and uncertainty, I chose to anchor myself in God's Word, trusting that His healing was greater, gentler, and full of life.

I had faith. I didn't take the medication. I prayed.

At my three-month scan, the tumor was unchanged. At my six-month scan, it was *gone*. The technician was speechless. She was so stunned that she left the room, disappearing behind the curtain to pull up my previous records while I lay there on the table, waiting. When she returned, I asked her what was wrong. She explained, almost in disbelief, that there was no evidence of any tumor and she had needed to double-check that she was even looking in the right area. Tears streamed down my face. I told her, "I know you don't know me, but I'm a believer in Jesus Christ, and I know He healed me. It was Jesus." She became just as emotional as I was. And then she said something I'll never forget:

"I'm not a believer ... but this changes everything for me."

Eleven years later, since May 29, 2014, I have been tumor-free. Every single day, I wake up with gratitude in my heart. I am here because of Him. God had me the entire time. But He wasn't done writing my story.

A Flood, A Promise, and an Unexpected Invitation

Not long after my six-month scan, life threw another curveball our way. We had just returned from our daughter's basketball game in Orange County when we opened the door and stepped into water. Everywhere. A pipe had burst under our kitchen sink, flooding our home. I should have been devastated. I should have felt defeated. But I wasn't. Because I knew something deeper, something unshakable.

God is good. Always.

We called our insurance company, and they sent out a contractor named Peter. From the start, something about our conversations felt different. We talked about our faith, and he shared that his brother was a pastor.

One day, as we stood in the middle of my torn-up kitchen, I told him my story, the healing, the miracles, and the promise I had made to God. Tears welled in his eyes. He knew, just as I did, that only God could do something like this. Then, Peter asked me something that took me by surprise, "Would you come speak at my brother's church?" Without hesitation, I said, "Oh my goodness, yes! Absolutely!"

Fear, Faith, and a Language I Didn't Understand

The night of the service, my husband and I arrived at the church, a few cities away. Close friends came too, the ones who had walked beside me through my battle. As I sat in the front row, I felt something stir in my spirit. Then the service began. Everything, the sermon, the prayers, the worship, was in a language I didn't understand. Romanian. I knew my contractor was Romanian, but he failed to mention that his brother's church was too, and that Romanian was the language they spoke. A knot formed in my stomach. *God ... why am I here? How could I share my story if they wouldn't understand me? Had I misunderstood what He was asking of me?* One worship song, then another. All in their language. The doubt grew louder. I looked around at the congregation, at the beautiful split-level church, and felt so out of place. Then, something shifted. The next song began. And it was in English. A song I knew well: "Oceans (Where feet may fail)" by Hillsong Music.

In that instant, peace flooded over me. It was as if God was whispering, "I've got you. Don't be afraid. Just trust Me." And so I did. When they called my name, I walked onto that stage with a faith that was stronger than fear. And I spoke. I poured out my story. I spoke of the battle, the healing, the overwhelming presence of God in my darkest moments. I saw tears streaming down faces. I saw hands lifted in worship. I saw smiles that said, *I understand. I believe, too.* God's work, God's timing. After the service, Peter came up to me, laughing. "Oh, I forgot to tell you," he said. "They prefer to hear things in their language, but they all understand English." I stared at him in disbelief, then burst out laughing. *God, You sure do have a sense of humor.*

Peter led me to the back, where people lined up, one by one, to hug me, to share their own stories of faith, of healing, of the incredible love of God. I was overwhelmed. Humbled. In awe. As we drove home that night, I was quiet, letting it all settle in. God had opened the door. I had walked through it. I had done His work, even when I didn't understand. I knew, with every fiber of my being, that I would keep walking through every door he opened. He had been faithful. He had healed me. My life, every breath, was His. Now, in everything I do, I pray first. I ask for His guidance. I surrender to His will.

"For we walk by faith, not by sight." (2 Corinthians 5:7, NKJV)

Keep the Faith, Even When It Feels Like Everything Is Falling Apart: Next Steps to Live By

When you're in the middle of the battle, physically, emotionally, or spiritually, it's easy to feel forgotten or forsaken. But faith isn't about everything making sense, it's about trusting that God is working even in the dark. Your healing may not be instant, but it's unfolding. Hold on. Keep praying. Keep believing. Faith is the anchor that steadies you when the storm tries to shake you.

Trust Your Inner Voice—It's Been Planted There for a Reason

God often whispers through your intuition. When something doesn't feel right medically, emotionally, or spiritually, listen to that voice. You are not crazy. You are not weak. Your inner knowing is a divine gift, not to be ignored. Learning to trust it will guide you toward the next right step, even when the path ahead is unclear.

Be Your Own Advocate—You Are Worth Fighting For

No one will fight for your healing like *you* will. Whether it's with doctors, family, or even yourself, you have the right to speak up, ask questions, and make choices that honor your body, mind, and soul. Self-advocacy is not selfish; it's sacred. God gave you that voice. Use it and never forget ...

We are the light.

Be bright. Be bold.

Wherever you go. In everything you do, because

He is always with you.

Chapter 8

The Power of Adaptability: Surviving the Battle from Both Sides

By Dr. Charrisse Somme-Davis

"I CAN BE CHANGED BY WHAT HAPPENS TO ME. BUT I REFUSE TO BE REDUCED BY IT."[9] -MAYA ANGELOU

This chapter focuses on the resources needed to survive and then thrive after receiving a diagnosis of cancer. The content shares my experience from both sides of a cancer diagnosis as I traveled the continuum of cancer by being a supporter who became a patient who was blessed to become a survivor. My experiences also highlight the powerful lessons learned through adaptation and transformation that were curated by resilience, mindset, and a network of support. My intention is to educate the reader with key takeaways that transcend cancer and can be applied to any life challenge.

---

9   Quote attributed to Maya Angelou; original source unverified.

On March 21, 2003, everything about my life as I had known it had changed with three words. It didn't matter that I had just gotten married ten months prior or that my husband and I had just closed on our first home. I remember the words reverberating in my mind, "You have cancer." I sat in disbelief, unable to process or respond to the doctor as he shared this information. While I sat in his examination room, suddenly chilled to the bone, I felt exhausted as I had emotionally traveled through the five stages of grief: denial, anger, bargaining, depression, and acceptance.

I tried to gather my thoughts, but one thought permeated my mind: uncertainty. Are they sure? *Did my testing get mixed up with someone else? Am I going to die? How did this happen, because I've never been a smoker?* In that moment, I had more questions than answers, trying to figure out the next steps, while knowing my future may not be something I needed to consider. Confusion clouded my mind as I transitioned from being the anchor in the storm of cancer, supporting my father, to the patient bearing my own diagnosis. In that shift, I recognized that many things had changed in a matter of minutes. From supporter to patient was unexpected and shocking. From patient to a survivor would require a different reaction and response.

As a caregiver, I felt confident in my abilities to learn all the tasks needed to be an effective supporter. Initially, I did not know what to expect, nor was I prepared for the responsibility associated with this role. I became educated about the regimen of care, which included medication schedules, appointments for scans, meetings with the doctors, medical terminology, coordinating nutritional meals, and ensuring environmental cleanliness, which included limiting interactions with others to prevent the spread of germs. Learning how to complete these tasks was essential to my father's care and survival. My father's calm demeanor and positive attitude made it easy to be patient and empathetic. His disposition also helped to decrease my worry, especially during doctor visits when glances and non-verbal communication told me more than I wanted to know.

Cancer was never supposed to be my story. I was the supporter, the one who said, "Everything is going to be okay," even when I wasn't sure that healing would be the outcome. I thought I understood cancer, but I had only known it from the outside. Being a supporter allowed me to attain knowledge and to be the guide, but it did not prepare me for the vulnerability of the diagnosis. Fortunately for me, my father was the visual reminder of faith is the assured expectation of things hoped for, and the evidence of things not seen (Hebrews 11:1).

Going from supporter to patient to survivor was a full-circle cancer journey that garnered a testimony of endurance. The experience placed me in a position to be an advocate, a learner, and a coach. Being a caregiver was something that I desired to do to help my father and our family. Fortunately, we had an existing network of support that was willing to help when needed to fill in any gaps that were present, whether it was for prayer, addressing personal care needs, transportation, or meal preparation. Having a network of support lessened the load and minimized the chances of anyone experiencing caregiver burnout.

As a therapist, I understood the danger of caregiver burnout, and I was very familiar with the term "wounded healer." Although I knew the focus needed to remain on my father, I believed that the challenge for the tribe was to stay encouraged, energized, and continually restored. While engaging in this labor of love, I sought God, as God was and is the well that never runs dry. I turned to my expertise and engaged in self-care practices that included living with gratitude, journaling my thoughts, and taking time away from caregiving. These practices gave me an opportunity to recharge and reflect while cognitively restructuring my mindset. Accepting help from the network and executing the above-mentioned strategies were beneficial for all of us.

I watched my father never have a bad day during all his trials. Looking back on it, that was amazing after I had become educated about his prognosis and all the challenges he was facing. You must understand that my dad was a jokester. He loved to laugh, and he was the type of person who never met a stranger. Every day, he would engage in conversation, which would transition to telling a joke in the middle of a conversation, and then he would crack up laughing at his own joke. Even though his voice was raspy and high-pitched because doctors had to scrape his esophagus during surgery to remove the cancer cells that had traveled from his lung, that did not deter him from experiencing joy. His behavior was such a definitive example of resilience. My father did not allow his circumstances to dictate how he lived. He truly was demonstrating a remarkable trait by adapting to the challenging life experience and opting to be hopeful about his future.

Having watched my father recover, I knew that he possessed a mindset to cope with and manage his cancer diagnosis. I wanted to believe that I was made of that same stuff so that I could manage my own health crisis. I continually repeated, "I can be changed by what happens to me. But I refuse to be reduced by it."[10] This was my affirmation. From diagnosis to remission, my father's attitude remained the same, cool and confident. His mindset allowed him to perceive that my recovery was certain. His attitude and actions convinced me that I was going to be okay. His ability to cultivate his mindset by embracing challenges and reframing how he viewed situations helped me to maintain a positive outlook. Being a patient is an entity that you can't quantify. I remember being stuck trying to figure out how this happened, as I was desperately looking for an experience or a circumstance to justify how I got cancer. I blamed the two sick buildings that I had worked at, where asbestos used to fall from the ceiling. I'm amused every time I drive by those sick buildings, which are now luxury condos.

During my nine months of treatment, which consisted of both chemotherapy and radiation, I felt strong enough to explore alternatives and remedies that could improve my overall wellness after treatment. I engaged in practices of colonic, which were colon irrigation flushes. I had ion foot baths to pull the toxins from my body, and based on the organ toxins that were pulled from, the salt water would turn a specific color. I also regulated my food choices and got massages regularly to support my lymphatic system. It helped that my mother became my personal chef and

---

10   Quote attributed to Maya Angelou; original source unverified.

cooked cancer-fighting foods. These efforts were crucial as I was diagnosed with Hodgkin's Lymphoma, which is a blood cancer resulting in me having a tumor in my chest. I was blessed that my husband had great insurance, thus, finances were not a burden, which is another way this wicked disease distresses a cancer patient during treatment and after treatment has ended.

Finances are a perfect example that demonstrates why we need to be resilient, why we must cultivate our minds to focus on our wellness, and why we need our network present to remind us of these things. Sometimes the emotional weight of cancer can feel heavier than the physical symptoms. I was lucky in some respects that I did not experience the typical side effects of traditional treatment. For example, I didn't lose weight, nor did I lose my hair. After treatment, I didn't experience nausea or a metallic taste in my mouth. In fact, my network and I went out to eat lunch each time after having treatment. As I became stronger, I reflected often. I leaned heavily on God's promise and his word, specifically Psalm 121:1-2 (KJV): "I will lift up mine eyes unto the hills from whence cometh my help. My help cometh from the Lord, which made heaven and earth."

Nothing can prepare you for the shock of hearing a cancer diagnosis if the diagnosis belongs to you or a loved one. It was scary for me when I thought about all the information I retained about cancer, which helped me to support my father through the process twice. It is humbling when you receive a diagnosis and begrudgingly travel down that same road, being re-traumatized and reliving the experience. Because of God, I shifted from victim to victorious because my mindset allowed me to rewrite the narrative. The Way Maker provided me with so many paths to promise, it was overwhelming. Not only did God allow me to live, but he also blessed me with a beautiful child who gave me purpose and a reason to live. This, of course, was after treatment and being told that childbearing was no longer an option for me. Because of my father, I became resilient when tested by cancer. He showed me that it is truly mind over matter. And because of my mother, I was able to rebuild my body and experience the sustaining encouragement of a network that became my circle of support. Having an existing network of support is amazing, and if you don't have one, creating a network is necessary. Because of my wonderful husband, I was able to focus on my wellness and experience the love that God created for a man and his wife.

Challenges come in a variety of ways. You don't have to be diagnosed with cancer to apply these powerful lessons. Any life crisis, such as divorce or a job loss, requires the same tools:

Resilience – to face uncertainty and continue to persevere.

Mindset – to shape the narrative by reframing your thinking to reclaim your power.

Support – exercise self-compassion and build community, as there is strength in togetherness.

Aside from using these tools, remember that faith puts the fire of fear out.

Chapter 9

My Battle with Breast Cancer: From Survivor to Thriver, from Dandelion to Iris

By Deborah (Debbie) Jenkins

"FOR I KNOW THE PLANS I HAVE FOR YOU," DECLARES THE LORD, "PLANS TO PROSPER YOU AND NOT TO HARM YOU, PLANS TO GIVE YOU HOPE AND A FUTURE." JEREMIAH 29:11 (NIV)

In Scarlet Hiltibidal's book, *Anxious: Fighting Anxiety With the Word of God*, she explains, "We live in a broken, sad, scary place. There is plenty to be anxious about."[11] She includes cancer as being anxiety-producing. I experienced anxiety and fear of the unknown, and of an unknown future, as well as depression when I got the diagnosis and ongoing afterwards. I experienced the feeling that this is the end of my time here on earth. I coped with all these feelings in a myriad of ways.

We may fear the future when we hear the word cancer. Will this be the end of my journey on this earth? Will I have

---

11 Scarllet Hilitibidal, *Anxious: Fighting Anxiety With the Word of God* (Nashville: LifeWay Press, 2021).

a recurrence if I do survive? Recurrence is a big fear no one really talks about. Also, anxiety may be caused by trauma. Cancer and recovery are a traumatic experience. Anxious thoughts on hearing the diagnosis of the C word are normal. I experienced anxiety and depression during and after cancer. I have taken steps towards overcoming, not just being a survivor but a thriver. I've learned that flowers, even dandelions, have a purpose. We all have a purpose here on earth. The iris is considered a flower of hope.

This has been my go-to verse in times of trouble or heartbreak:

"For I know the plans I have for you," declares the Lord, "plans to prosper you and not to harm you, plans to give you hope and a future." (Jeremiah 29:11, NIV)

Having a cancer diagnosis is very traumatizing. Reading scripture has helped me through the roller coaster of cancer. The roller coaster doesn't end after one surgery. It goes on from the moment of the diagnosis to endless tests and doctor visits.

Another go-to verse for me is Psalm 22. When the psalmist David in the Bible was going through a hard trial, he wrote:

"My God, my God, why have you forsaken me?
Why are you so far from saving me, so far from my cries of anguish?
My God, I cry out by day, but you do not answer, by night, but I find no rest."
(Psalm 22:1-2, NIV)

It may feel like this when we are given a diagnosis of cancer. We may feel afraid and hopeless, anxious and depressed. My Grandmother got the diagnosis of breast cancer in the 1970s. She went to her car and cried and screamed. She died at the age of fifty-six.

My traumatic roller coaster began on September 28, 2023, when I was given a diagnosis of stage 1 breast cancer. I had gone in for a routine mammogram. I was overdue. After the mammogram, the doctor called in and said they found something suspicious and referred me to an oncologist specialist for further testing. There was a small lump found in my right breast. It turned out to be a malignant cancerous tumor. I remember feeling like I was in a tunnel; it felt surreal, like it couldn't be happening.

I was referred to an oncologist and a breast surgeon. From there, I had a biopsy of the tumor. An MRI and an ultrasound were done to determine the size of the tumor and whether it had metastasized. Thankfully, it hadn't spread, and it was small, less than two centimeters.

My mother was given a diagnosis of breast cancer over the phone in 1995. She felt as if she was in shock. She underwent a mastectomy with reconstruction at the age of 60. Today, she is a ten-year survivor.

My Grandmother's and Mother's ordeal prompted me to have genetic testing ten years ago. It came back positive for the BRCA 2 gene, which means my risk of getting cancer is high. The BRCA protein, also known as breast cancer type 2 susceptibility protein, is a crucial part of the DNA repair process. When there is a mutation (or change) in the

BRCA2 gene, it can increase the risk of developing certain cancers, including breast cancer, which can be passed down from parents to children. I had a high risk and opted for a hysterectomy years ago. It was suggested that I have a preventative mastectomy at the time, like the actress Angelina Jolie, but I held off. Years later, I would be diagnosed with cancer. Did I make the right decision in not having preventive surgery? Maybe not, but at least I knew for sure. I had regular mammograms and MRIs and took preventative measures with regular checkups. It is a personal decision to have the surgery when having a diagnosis of a cancer gene. I had a full hysterectomy, which significantly lessened ovarian cancer risk.

It's been almost two years since I was given a breast cancer diagnosis. Five years is considered remission, but I feel like I'm surviving and thriving after two. Like a flower in bloom, like a beautiful Iris, like a dandelion, I am thriving. Even a dandelion has a purpose. I am discovering my purpose. Sometimes, a traumatic experience can push us closer to our destiny.

My faith in Christ has seen me through many trials and tribulations. I became a Christian at the age of twenty and was baptized at the age of twenty-three. My faith has helped me through the diagnosis of breast cancer and three surgeries, as well as helping through back surgery and heart surgery.

The breast surgeon recommended a bilateral mastectomy because I have the BRCA2 gene. I also had an MRI and an ultrasound to see if the cancer metastasized (spread to other parts of the body). Thankfully, it did not.

My surgery was postponed due to a bladder infection, and I was placed on antibiotics. Waiting was very hard, because it's the fear of the unknown and the surgery itself.

On September 28, 2023, I went for a bilateral skin-sparing mastectomy with right sentinel lymph node biopsy and tissue expander reconstruction. Expanders were put in, and I would later have implants. I asked the surgeon if doing both together was safe, and she replied it would be fine, but it wasn't. I was rushed to the hospital for a pneumothorax (a small tear in my lung). The plastic surgeon had gone too deep and nicked my lung. I was rushed to the emergency hospital, where I spent a week in recovery. Afterwards, I spent a week in a rehab facility. It was a horrible experience, made worse by drains put in the breasts by surgeons.

The doctor was unable to put in an expander on the right, and it would be a few months before I had another surgery, and a third surgery weeks later. After that, I opted for no more surgeries.

After surgeries, doctors put in drains in the breasts so blood would collect. The drains had to be changed and measured every few hours. That was very uncomfortable. It was almost the worst part of the whole surgery. It was hard to sleep. They were removed after a couple of weeks once the blood was no longer draining. I stayed with my dear cousin after a couple of surgeries, and my parents helped in the recovery.

I went to see my oncologist, who prescribed an anti-cancer drug, Arimidex, and Prolia (a six-month shot for bone density). I was diagnosed with Osteoporosis. I have been afraid to take these because of some of the side effects.

Following doctors' orders is important. He also suggested vitamin D and calcium supplements. Brittle bones are a possibility, so taking supplements and weight-bearing exercises is very important.

My doctor and I decided I should take Anastrozole and Fosamax (a once-a-week pill for bone density). Also, vitamin D and calcium.

A special test, CA125, was done to determine if I needed chemo or radiation. If the number was below 26, I would need chemotherapy. If above 26, I would not. It was above 26, and I did not need chemotherapy or radiation.

When people are told they have the C word, I believe we go through five stages of grief: Denial, Anger, Bargaining, Depression, and Acceptance. At first, I was in disbelief, almost like being in a tunnel. There has to be a mistake, or it can't be serious, I believed. However, people should not put their feelings in a box. We are all different, and the five stages are not an all and all for everyone.

New Beginnings

A couple of years later, I am doing okay, but no one told me about the anxiety and depression I would go through post-cancer.

Anxiety and sometimes panic attacks rear their ugly head. It's an ongoing battle for me. Many experience these feelings post-cancer.

> "Therefore do not worry about tomorrow, for tomorrow will worry about itself. Each day has enough trouble of its own." (Matthew 6:34, NIV)

"Do not be anxious about anything, but in every situation, by prayer and petition, with thanksgiving, present your requests to God." (Philippians 4:6, NIV)

Cancer sufferers are a sisterhood that I never wanted to be in. I have met and talked to quite a few who have or are undergoing cancer. I watch many YouTube videos for encouragement and therapy. I particularly like Therapy in a Nutshell. Live therapy sessions are beneficial. Some may need antidepressants to help cope. Enjoying nature and walking (exercising) helps. Joining support groups with other cancer survivors is beneficial. I joined an online group entitled Frederick Pink Warriors. They meet for lunch once a month. I joined a ladies' group that meets for lunch every two weeks called Frederick Ladies Who Eat. Maintaining a social life is very important to recovery. A sense of belonging is very important.

I have joined a wonderful online church called Father Heart Church that has been a great support for me during and after cancer. They meet every night online and have interactive bible studies, deliverance and healing sessions, small group meetings, and Sunday services. They also have amazing care callers, who take the time to talk and care. All of this has helped me in my healing journey. It has helped me with anxiety and depression, which can come on like a thief on a clear sunny day. Many people struggle with this post-cancer. Cancer and recovery take a long time and are ongoing.

As the psalmist David wrote in the bible,

"I love the Lord, for he heard my voice; he heard my cry for mercy.

Because he turned his ear to me, I will call on him as long as I live.
The cords of death entangled me, and the anguish of the grave came over me;
I was overcome by distress and sorrow,
Then I called on the name of the Lord: "Lord, save me!" (Psalm 116:1-4, NIV)

And He did!

Like the iris, which blooms and symbolizes hope, I have put my hope in God.

Next Steps

Eating healthy during and after a cancer diagnosis is very important! Post-cancer does not mean stop taking care of oneself. Cancer recovery is an ongoing process. Recovering does not mean going back to eating processed, chemical-laden junk food. Dr. Amy Morris (who has many videos on YouTube and is a Cancer survivor) suggests eating berries, especially blueberries, nuts, and seeds like flax seeds. Walnuts are very good for brain health, too.

Dr. Amy also suggests lean protein like organic Chicken, wild-caught salmon, and tuna, which are a good source of Omega 3.

A diet rich in fruits, vegetables, whole grains, and legumes (beans) is associated with a lower cancer risk. The healthiest foods are pesticide-free organic foods.

A contributing factor to cancer recurrence, which can cause anxiety and depression, is stress. We should be careful to maintain a healthy lifestyle, keeping stress to a minimum by exercising and eating healthy. Two things I do to limit stress are walking and journaling. Writing down my thoughts and making it clear on paper has helped me. "My heart is stirred by a noble theme as I recite my verses for the king; my tongue is the pen of a skillful writer." (Psalm 45:1 NIV).

I put my hope in God and the Trinity to see me through, as I did during my lengthy treatment and recovery. I will always have hope. (see Psalms 71:14 and Jeremiah 29:11)

A new all-natural solution to depression and anxiety is called Zen Drops. This has not been approved by a doctor, so please continue to follow a doctor. Zen drops' primary ingredient comes from a natural plant source used around the Mediterranean for centuries. Zen drops boost mood and happiness, improve anxiety, focus, and memory. It triggers the release of anandamide and Z-arachidonoylglycerol. YouTube video.

As stated, taking vitamin D3 and getting nutrition from foods like magnesium and potassium foods is very good. Iron supplementation is helpful. Please check with your healthcare provider to determine vitamin levels and appropriate dosages.

Like an Iris flower, I will continue to press on to the race God has for me. Through proper nutrition, exercise, supportive groups, church fellowship, journaling, and scriptures, I will press on to the goal God has for me. I will continue to have hope and forge forward into my cancer recovery and the goal and purpose God has for me.

About the Authors

*

Kalindi L. Garvin

Kalindi Garvin is a writer, career strategist, and cancer survivor who believes in the quiet power of persistence and presence. She directs Engineering Career Services at the University of Iowa and is the founder of Career Communication Strategies. A certified Master Resume Writer and mother of four, Kalindi draws from her journey through illness, young widowhood, and rediscovery to help others find meaning and voice in their own stories. Her writing explores themes of identity, resilience, and the beauty woven into ordinary moments. She lives in Iowa, where she's always looking for glimmers of light—on trails, in stories, and in life.

Connect with Kalindi:
https://substack.com/@kalindigarvin

Heather Hetchler, MA

Heather Hetchler, MA is a certified relationship coach, speaker, writer, cancer survivor and reframing expert who helps midlife women face unexpected challenges with calm, clarity, and confidence. With over 15 years of experience, she guides clients through relational dynamics, empty nesting, health shifts, and personal transformation. Originally focused on stepfamilies, Heather now equips women in midlife to reclaim their divine purpose and peace. Heather lives in Cleveland with her husband, Andy, and their rescue dog—cheering on her four adult children and two adult stepchildren.

Connect with Heather:

heather@heatherhetchlercoaching.com

www.HeatherHetchlerCoaching.com

www.ReframingRelationships.com

Instagram: https://www.instagram.com/reframingrelationships/

LinkedIn: https://www.linkedin.com/in/heatherhetchler/
Facebook: https://www.facebook.com/ReframeYourRelationships

About the Authors

Page Geske

Page Geske is the author of Milepost 95 From Wreckage to Redemption—a powerful story of survival, faith and second chances. After narrowly escaping death in a 2007 car accident and conquering Stage 2A colon cancer in 2016, Page felt a deep calling to share her journey. With contagious hope and a fierce passion for life, she inspires both women and men to live boldly, love deeply, and never give up.

Today, Page thrives by embracing healthy living, daily movement and exercise, and a deep trust in the Lord's healing power. Cancer-free since 2017, she is a dedicated advocate for colon cancer awareness, believing that if her story can save even one life, it's worth every word.

Based in Boise, Idaho, Page cherishes time with her three grown sons and fills her days with outdoor adventures—hiking, biking, kayaking and snowshoeing alongside her spirited mini-Goldendoodle, Journey.

Connect with Page:
https://pagegeske.com

Amy McClain

Amy is married to one amazing man of God, mother to five outstanding young adults, homeschool mom, career tribal missionary, overcomer of thyroid cancer. Together with her family, they spent over a decade at the "ends of the earth," living among and ministering to indigenous people in the Papuan jungle. Her physical and spiritual journey with the uninvited companion of thyroid cancer taught her priceless lessons about overcoming anxiety about the future, doubting God's purpose, and looking for the hidden gifts of grace to be found in the long periods of waiting to understand His will.

Connect with Amy:

https://amyjareb.com/
Email: amy@amyjareb.com
Instagram: https://www.instagram.com/amyjareb

About the Authors

Julie Stapleton

Julie Stapleton is a Christian, a wife to the most wonderful and supportive husband, Michael, a mother of two boys, Brennan and Mason, a daughter, a sister, and a friend. Julie served 5 years in the United States Navy as a hospital corpsman and has been an Emergency Room Nurse for 26 years and a teacher for 2 years. During COVID, Julie was a travel nurse in Boston and North Dakota. Julie was diagnosed with HER2+ breast cancer in 2024 and, after undergoing chemotherapy and a bilateral mastectomy, is cancer-free. She will soon begin radiation and the reconstructive process.

Connect with Julie:

Facebook: https://www.facebook.com/julie.woodstapleton
Instagram: https://www.instagram.com/jstapleton0814

Susan Laurie Hutchinson

Susan Laurie Hutchinson lives in Bucks County, Pennsylvania, with her husband Mike, whom she refers to in her blog as "The Builder." They have three children, 11 grandchildren, 2 great-grandchildren, lots of laughs, hopes, and dreams. As a survivor of many years of stage 4 ovarian cancer, Susan is a full-time woman of hope. She has been a speaker for Stonecroft Ministries and founded Hanging on Hope, a subscription box for women diagnosed with cancer. Finding the blessing in each God-given day is why she can laugh without fear of the future.

Connect with Susan:

www.hangingonhope.com
Facebook: https://www.facebook.com/hangingonhopebox
Instagram: https://www.instagram.com/hangingonhope-box

About the Authors

Julie O'Dell

Julie O'Dell is an actor, writer and survivor whose journey through illness, faith and healing has touched countless lives. In A Divine Orchestration: My Journey Through Fear, Faith and Healing, she shares her powerful testimony of overcoming fear, embracing faith, and experiencing a miraculous recovery. A devoted Mother and passionate storyteller, she uses her voice to inspire others to trust in divine timing and power of resilence. Through her work in both writing and acting, she hopes to encourage those facing their own battles, reminding them the light can ALWAYS break through the darkness.

Connect with Julie:
www.juliedoesvoiceover.com
Instagram: https://www.instagram.com/joyfulheartjules

Dr. Charrisse Somme-Davis

Wife and mother of one, Charrisse Somme-Davis, Ed.D, LCMHCS is an entrepreneur, licensed counselor and educator who is active within her community. Currently, she serves as a Community Advisory Board member for Atrium Health Wake Forest Baptist Comprehensive Cancer Center. A two-time HBCU graduate, she is the Chief Operating Officer at Still Family, LLC that provides services and support for those individuals diagnosed with an Intellectual Disability, and sole proprietor of Premier Counseling Professionals, which is a private practice offering counseling, coaching, and consultative services to individuals, groups, and organizations.

Connect with Charrisse:

https://pcpresponds.com/

LinkedIn: www.linkedin.com/in/charrisse-somme-ed-d-lcmhcs-6b088355

Deborah (Debbie) Jenkins

Deborah is a senior caregiver, a retired medical assistant (CMA), medical transcriptionist, and an insurance rater, but has never forgotten her first love of writing. She began writing in grade school, receiving A's in English and writing. Math not so much. She writes fiction and nonfiction. She wrote a children's book entitled *Owen, the Ugly Bird*, and a short story entitled "Jacklin: More Than a Friend" in sixth grade. She was second in a spelling bee contest in sixth grade, setting a course for her writing. Being an avid reader and writer her whole life led to her love of writing and hopes of becoming a published author.

Closing

Dear Reader,

Thank you for reading *Beyond the Battle: Cancer Survivors' Stories of Resilience, Recovery, and Hope!*

I want to take a moment to celebrate the incredible authors who contributed to this meaningful book. They have poured their hearts into discovering, clarifying, and sharing their unique messages—and now, you get to benefit from their hard work and dedication.

At hope*books, we are deeply proud of our authors and are honored to partner with them on this journey. If you've ever considered writing and publishing your book, we invite you to visit hopebooks.com to learn more about our coaching and publishing services. We believe that everyone has a message to share and an audience to serve, and the world needs your hopeful words now more than ever.

Once again, let's take a moment to celebrate the hard work of these authors in bringing *Beyond the Battle* to life.

Sincerely,

Brian Dixon

Publisher, hope*books

Looking to *connect* with a community of writers?

hope * writers
www.hopewriters.com

The world needs your *hope-filled* words more now than ever before.

Thinking about *writing* your own book?

hope * books
www.hopebooks.com

Made in the USA
Columbia, SC
06 June 2025

285aa7eb-cbdc-48e1-800e-bdd2ebbb90b1R01